The Heart of England Way

by John Roberts

WALKWAYS

by walkers .....for walkers

****
WALKWAYS
John Roberts
67 Cliffe Way, Warwick
CV34 5JG   01926 776363
****

THE
HEART OF ENGLAND
WAY

described by John Roberts

ISBN 0 947708 40 5

First Published 1980 (Thornhill Press)
Second Edition 1982 (Thornhill Press)
Map Sheet Edition 1989 (WALKWAYS)
Fourth Edition 1990 (WALKWAYS)
Fifth Edition 1995 (WALKWAYS)
Sixth Edition 2000 (WALKWAYS)

WALKWAYS

by walkers.....for walkers

DaywalkS Footpath Networks
Networks of linked paths covering an area.

Cannock Chase (£4.95)
Vale of Llangollen (£4.95)
Wyre Forest (£4.95)

Strolls & Walks
From each place there is a short stroll and a walk.

Strolls & Walks from Picnic Places (Midlands) (£4.95)
Strolls & Walks from Cotswold Villages (£6.45)
Strolls & Walks from Midland Villages ((£5.75)

Long Distance Routes
Step by step guides in both directions

Warwickshire's Centenary Way (£6.95)
North Worcestershire Path & Midland Link (£5.75)
Birmingham to Aberystwyth (1999)
Llangollen to Snowdon (1999)
Birmingham to Bala (some time)

Walks around ...
Walks in specific areas by Ramblers Association groups.

Twenty Walks around Rugby (£4.95)
Ten Walks around Coventry (£3.95)
Walks around Stourbridge (£4.75)

**67 Cliffe Way, Warwick
CV34 5JG Tel/Fax 01926 776363
(write or phone for catalogue)**

i

Contents

Revised Edition

The 5th edition of the Heart of England Way guide issued in 1995 was entirely new. It was needed because of some major changes to the route and many minor ones, such as main roads renumbered, cooling towers demolished, a post box moved and a farm demolished. There have been no big route changes in the five years since it came out, but there have been a surprising number of footpath diversions, new fences, trees removed and more happily, trees planted. This edition is therefore an updated version of the last with new photos.

This emphasises the importance of my Amendment Service under which you can get a free cumulative updating slip simply by phoning for it. All I ask in return is that you tell me if you come upon any point at which the directions do not make sense. Believe me, they did when they were written, and when they don't it is usually because something has altered. I don't know if phoning me is a big effort or a ghastly experience, but amazingly few people bother.

Apart from the directions, I have altered some of the early pages of the book to show my new address and phone/fax number. The section, *Using the Guide* now includes a short glossary to explain what I mean by terms like 'half right' or 'bear right'. The list of *Starting Points* has been reorganised from alphabetical to route order and includes wayside pubs. Thank you again to those observant people who have sent me their observations on the last book, and I hope the postman continues to bring me (mostly) complimentary letters.

John Roberts
December 1999

Meet the Heart
of England Way

Later you can read the full description of the Way - views,
churches, woods and ponds. In these sections I want to sketch
general impressions of a route which I have come to like very
much, the West Midland's own Long Distance Footpath at the
end of the back garden.

The basic facts about the Way are that it is a Regional Long
Distance Path recognised by the three County Councils and
one Borough Council through whose areas it passes: Staffordshire, Warwickshire Gloucestershire and Solihull MBC.
It runs almost 100 miles from Milford on the northern tip
of Cannock Chase to Bourton on the Water in the Cotswolds
and links the Staffordshire Way, Centenary Way, Cotswold
Way, Oxfordshire Way and the Thames Path.

From the Chase the Way curves south-east via Lichfield to
the Tame Valley, then south-west through Meriden and Henley
in Arden to Alcester, circling the eastern side of Birmingham
but passing west of Coventry. The lower section runs south,
more or less, across the Vale of Evesham and the northern
Cotswold Hills to Bourton on the Water.

The Staffordshire Way and Cotswold Way have long been
recognised as "official" Long Distance Paths, and the Oxfordshire Way and Thames Path more recently. The Staffs
Way was created by the County Council and the Cotswold
from an idea by members of the Ramblers Association which
was soon adopted by Gloucestershire County Council. By
contrast it took twelve years of solid effort by the Heart of
England Way Association to win recognition for this route,
which was only achieved in 1990.

Warwickshire CC did not at that time have a policy to create
a Long Distance Path and perhaps hesitated because of a
striking feature of the Heart of England Way, one of its

main virtues. It runs through a most pleasant landscape with many beautiful views and in places feels deeply rural, but it does run around the eastern rim of one of the world's biggest concentrations of people and industry. Perhaps this was not felt to be a place where anyone would want a Long Distance Footpath, they belong in National Parks. But it turned out that people did want one - and right next door.

Warwickshire County Council have become so attached to this idea that they paid us the implied compliment of creating an LDP of their own. The Centenary Way (1991) celebrates the County Council's own origin in 1894 and encircles the county, visiting most of the notable places and sites and joining the HofEW at both ends. They make a nice 196 mile circuit.

The Heart of England Way itself is not in the least urban, but is often in distant view or earshot of the sights and sounds of civilisation. I find this mixture of the deeply rural with urban fringe attractive and fascinating. I can reach the Way easily by bus or train for a day's walking, and as easily return from another place in the evening.

You will see the big silver birds cruising to Elmdon air-port, graceful as the swans at Kingsbury Water Park. Bulgy old propellor aircraft bustle bellies full of cargo to Baginton airport while ducks upend in a pond. There are church spires amongst the trees and the odd pylon.

From high points in the Meriden area is an outstanding, exciting view of the centre of the great city of Birmingham, miles away, a vast group of tall white buildings on top of a plateau. This is the Midlands where people live and work, there is no need to pretend it is the Lake District - it has its own value.

Landscapes

This is a broad brush impression of the varying landscapes from north to south.

Cannock Chase is known to people in the Midlands but is usually a surprise for other visitors. Here in the middle of gently rolling green fields is a sandy, pebbly plateau of heathland, with birch, heather, bilberry and bracken spread over small, steep hills. To the south are large plantations of Scots and Corsican pine. Castle Ring is an Iron Age fort on the highest point at the southern tip.

Heading south towards Lichfield, the Way falls gently through mixed farmland into a broad, flat bottomed valley. The next section to Weeford across Packington Moor is again sandy heath and obviously related to the Chase, though the fact is disguised by farming.

From Weeford for over a mile is a delightful group of small grassy Alps. They are quite alone up here and you will not see similar contours until south of Henley in Arden.

The Way soon turns east and descends very gently into the Tame Valley, then travels up it along the Birmingham & Fazeley Canal to Kingsbury. Here is the fascinating Water Park created from disused gravel pits at river level. After this broad, watery area comes miles of pleasant Midlands farmscape, with trees, crops and cattle, rising and falling to Shustoke Reservoir. The general character of the farming and the scenery remains much the same for another mile or so, until perhaps Dumble Wood.

South of the wood there is a subtle change which you sense as you cross the big arable field between Shawbury and Heach Woods. Cross the stile where the two woods nearly

meet, and you are on grassland and rising, with shapely
small hills, more woods and more sheep; this is the
Arden landscape.

The Forest of Arden really has the leading role in Shakespeare's *Midsummer Night's Dream*, a spell woven out of
Eden and Arcadia by rather sexy faries. The section south
to Henley is a lovely procession of English villages and
mellow churches, with a moated Tudor manor house at
Baddlesley Clinton. The Way literally dives into Henley
in Arden from a steep sided iron age fort.

Warwickshire is no longer so leafy as people think,
especially since the destructive arrival of the elm bark
beetle. The County has some 3% tree cover compared
with 6 or 7% in Worcestershire, Shropshire and Staffordshire. This is one reason why Warwickshire County
Council launched the *New Forest of Arden* project, which
is a concerted drive to plant and encourage planting of
150 million trees in this 250 square mile area. The HoEW
Association has planted small groups of trees at selected
points along the Way.

From Henley to Alcester is more hilly as the Way crosses
the Alne Hills in the triangle between the rivers Alne and
Arrow. South of Alcester, for a while, it seems as though
Arden will continue, but once over the hump of Oversley
Hill the Way falls into the valley of the River Arrow.

The valley widens and the farming becomes more arable
and the landscape flat and willowy. After Broom you are
in the market garden country of the Vale of Evesham
and you soon cross the River Avon at Bidford.

After a riverside episode the route rises and for the next
couple of miles you walk through prosperous vegetables
and soft fruit bushes. Then you climb slightly to leave
the Vale and from Dorsington to Lower Quinton it is
again flat, mixed farming country.

Meon Hill rises from this broad, level fieldscape, a green whale and a northern outlier of the Cotswolds. The Way crosses its southern flank to fall again briefly into glass-house country at Mickleton. But immediately after the village, without even passing the church, you know from the wooded hills that you have reached the Cotswolds. The steep ridge of Bakers Hill carries you on towards Chipping Campden.

Rising slowly into the north Cotswolds, the Way crawls over the shoulders of long hills and down steep green valleys. The walls, the houses and churches and the stones in the fields are honey and grey. This is limestone country and the Cotswolds are part of the great Jurassic ridge between Dorset and the Humber. Passing Batsford Arboretum the Way falls gently through the parkland of Sezincote, the great house with its huge oriental dome in full view. Following clear, fast Cotswold streams the Way continues to fall through the Swells and Lower Slaughter to Bourton on the Water.

One of the happiest features of the British landscape is its variety. In this 100 miles we can show you sandy heath, rolling grassland, the woods and pastures of Arden, the rich plain of the Avon and limestone hills.

Cannock Chase and Berkswell Park

The Way it Was

by John Watts
Heart of England Way Association

The Heart of England Way sprang out of an idea from the Alcester Civic Society. Responding to a questionaire from Warwickshire County Council about use of footpaths, they wrote a paper proposing that some paths across the County be treated as key routes, with circular walks from these arteries.

There was no response, so in 1978 the Society decided to promote their own route. They invited rambling clubs to join in and formed a committee with delegates from Alcester Civic Society, Wootten Wawen Footpaths Group, Shirley Rambling Club, Lichfield Group of the Ramblers Association, North Warwicks Rambling Club, Heart of England Rambling Club, Coventry CHA, Coventry HF, and Stratford upon Avon group of the RA.

At first the Committee agreed the objective of a route conn-ecting Lichfield to Chipping Campden, the eastern end of the Cotswold Way. Each club was asked to find a route over a 10 mile section between given start and finishing points, such as Henley in Arden to Alcester. Quite soon they decided to extend the route and link the Cotswold Way with the Staffordshire Way on Cannock Chase.

At first we called the route the West Warwickshire Way, but it soon became Heart of England Way. By 1979 routes surveyed by the clubs had been agreed and a continuous 80 mile regional footpath created, at least on paper. It was put to the County Councils - Staffordshire, Warwickshire, West Midlands and Gloucestershire, but only the latter showed any interest.

There were obstructions, missing footbridges and many other problems, with very few waymarks. In 1979 the Committee decided to write a guide, which was published by Thornhill Press. For several years they persisted in trying to get the route recognised by the Counties, the NFU and others, but without much sucess. In Warwickshire there were not even sufficient resources to clear obstructions.

Once again the Committee took the initiative and in 1982 started talking to the farmers and landowners. At last there was some progress in building stiles, up to fifty over a few years. Some obstructions were cleared and waymarks placed. Parish Councils were consulted and most of them supported the idea. Then in the late 1980's the Countryside Commission took an influential interest, and Warwickshire County Council began to respond, building bridges and supplying stiles. A liasion committee was formed to act as a forum for the interests of farmers, landowners and walkers.

It was a long story of enthusiatic amateurs persisting for ten years and finally being rewarded by official recognition of the Way by the County Councils: Staffordshire, Gloucestershire and Warwickshire, and Solihull Borough.

Members still work to publicise, maintain and upgrade the Way through a well organised voluntary path warden service which liases with farmers and makes regular inspections. We have contributed to Warwickshire's *New Forest of Arden* scheme by planting groups of trees along the Way. All this work is almost entirely financed from members subscriptions and royalties from sales of the the guide.

We are affiliated to The Ramblers and the Long Distance Walkers Association, and members include individuals and clubs. Why not join us and help to improve and promote the Way - it only costs £4.00.

Please send your cheque to Sheila Carter
50, George Road, Water Orton, Birmingham B46 1PE

Using the Guide

This guide gives full step by step directions for walking from North to South and South to North. The route is quite comprehensively waymarked, but waymarks and road signs are often damaged or disappear, so the directions are written as if they did not exist.

The route directions are quite separate from the description and comment, they are very terse, and set in short, narrow, numbered paragraphs in a clear and open typeface. These and less obvious features have been adopted for Walkways books after much thought. My aim to give information in easily located and remembered blocks of convenient size, bearing in mind that you will be reading on the move.

Distances in *yards* or *miles* are to give you a ROUGH idea how far to walk. You do not need to measure because you will be given something to look out for, such as a stile or gate. So if I say "go .6 mile to the old mill", you will not start to worry if you can't see the old mill, or whatever, after 200 yards. I use yards where I think you will know how far I mean, but few of us know what 600 yards look like, so for longer distances I turn to fractions of a mile.

Distances in *paces* are given to be COUNTED out if you need to. These are infrequent and only for a few yards at a time. Paces vary but you can allow for being tall or short. The reason for all this is that people carry a pace with them but not usually a measuring tape.

I have largely avoided abbreviations but certain phrases recur. You will sometimes see *half R* (or L) meaning a half turn, or about 45 degrees. Therefore *bear R* (or L) means a narrower angle than a half turn, or just tending away from straight ahead. A *road* has a tarmac surface and is usually big enough for a white line down the middle. *Lanes* are tarmaced but smaller and without white lines. *Drives* are like lanes but not public. *Tracks* are wide enough for a four wheeled vehicle and might have an earth, grass or stone surface. A *path* may have any surface, from mud to tarmac, but is only pedestrian width.

The maps are sketches to an approximate scale of 2.5ins/ 1mile and designed to confirm where you are rather than for route finding. The big black arrow on each map points north, but you had guessed as much, hadn't you.

Paragraph numbers also have letters: heading North (to Cannock Chase) - **(N123)**, heading South (to the Cotswolds) - **(S145)**. These appear at intervals on the maps, N numbers on the right and S on the left.

It might be helpful to carry Ordnance Survey Landranger (1.25ins/1mile) maps to help you find starting points, for general interest and if you want to leave the route to find an urgent dentist. Below I list the relevant Landranger sheets, and for people who are mad about maps, those of the Ordnance Survey Pathfinder (2.5ins/1mile) series.

The Heart of England waymarks are green and white discs bearing the oak trees logo. There should be waymarks where the Way leaves metalled roads, and overland when the occupier has allowed us to place them.

Where the published route does not follow a public right of way the path will be usually be marked with white arrows or other signs plus the HOEW disc. These sections are used with permission of landowners and occupiers with no intention to dedicate them as public rights of way.

Gloucestershire, Staffordshire and Warwickshire County Councils, Solihull Borough, the NFU and CLA have recognised the Way as a recreational footpath. However the route was pioneered entirely by the Association so any enquiries should be made direct to them.

Amendment Service

The countryside changes all the time. Paths are diverted, hedges removed, tracks, fences and barns come and go. To keep walk directions up to date I issue Amendment Slips - a unique and free service.

PHONE ME on 01926 776363 with with a note of the book(s) that you have and I will send you up to date Slips.

EVEN NEW or recently purchased books can suffer changes within weeks, it is always worth checking.

DON'T BOTHER copying changes into your book(s). Just dot affected paragraphs with highlighter and keep the Slips in the front of the plastic cover.

PLEASE WRITE, PHONE or FAX to report any changes or problems stating book, route and paragraph number.

Ordnance Survey Maps

Landranger Maps (1.50,000) (1.25 ins/mile) (2 cms/km)
127 Stafford 128 Derby 139 Birmingham 140 Leicester
150 Worcester 151 Stratford 163 Cheltenham.

Pathfinder Maps (1:25,000) (2.5 ins/mile) (4 cms/km)
850 SJ 82/92 Stafford, 871 SJ 81/91 Cannock(North),
872 SK 01/11 Rugeley, 892 SK 00/10, Lichfield,
914 SP 29/39 Nuneaton, 935 SP 28/38 Coventry (North),
955 SP 27/37 Coventry (South), 975 SP 06/16 Redditch,
997 SP 05/15 Stratford (West), 1020 SP 04/14 Evesham
1043 SP03/13 Broadway, 1067 SP02/12 Winchcombe.

Transport and Accommodation

ACCOMMODATION LIST
For a free and up to date list of hotels, bed & breakfast places and camp sites, phone 01926 776363. If you have to leave a message please give your phone number, name and address. In emergency I can fax the list to you.

RAIL
There are railway stations at Stafford, Lichfield, Henley in Arden and Moreton in Marsh (within reach of Bourton on the Hill). Train enquiries - 0345 484950.

BUSES
Each County Council has an information desk which can give comprehensive details of services, and in the list of Starting Points and Pubs I have noted their telephone numbers. Where a Starting Point has a bus service I have said so and indicated which number to ring.

CAR
You can motor to any of the starting points, but there is very limited parking space at some of them, as I note in the list. Use these points to be set down or picked up.

FEET
People planning to start from Milford can take a footpath route from Stafford. On the next page are directions for a pleasant river and canalside walk of 3.5 miles/5.6 kms from centre to centre.

LINKED LONG DISTANCE PATHS
Cannock Chase - *Staffordshire Way*, Kingsbury Water Park - *Centenary Way*, Chipping Campden - *Cotswold Way*, Bourton on the Water - *Oxfordshire Way*. My own recent addition is the *Midland Link*, which runs west from Kenilworth *(CW)* via Baddesley Clinton *(HoEW)* to the *North Worcestershire Path*, the *Staffs Way* and the *Worcestershire Way*.

Stafford to Milford

(1) Find traffic lights by Royal Bank of Scotland at junction of Greengate St & Bridge St. Go to bridge & join path with river ON YOUR L.

(2) Go downstream to 2nd footbridge & cross. Go R .5 mile to path end at road.

(3) Cross bridge, then road, & take steps down to rejoin river. Follow appx .5 mile to pylon & footbridge R.

(4) Cross bridge & go L to cross next bridge. Go L toward next pylon, to gate & road.

(5) Cross road & footpath & go R to join canal towpath. Go L appx 2.5 miles. After AQUEDUCT over Sow go to next bridge.

(6) Go R up steps to lane. Go ahead over river & railway to Milford Common. ●

Milford to Stafford

(a) Go to Shugborough end of Common (R of Fiat garage), & take lane.

(b) Cross railway & river to canal & join towpath. Go L appx 2.5 miles. Watch for line of chalets on far bank & go to next bridge (No.101 St Thomas).

(c) Go R onto road, follow it 25yds & take stile by gate NB pylon ahead & line of trees. Go to their R end.

(d) Cross bridge, go L & cross next bridge, then ahead to join riverside path.

(e) Go upstream with river on your R appx .5 miles to road.

(f) Cross bridge & road to rejoin river. Follow .5 mile (under 2 road bridges) to FOOTBRIDGE. Cross & go R to town.●

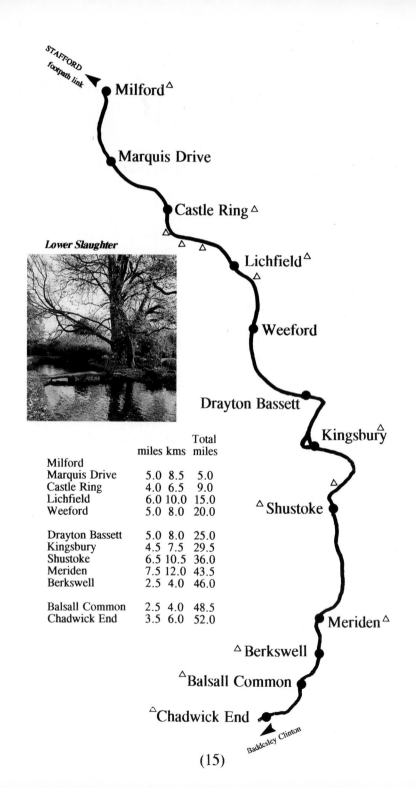

STAFFORD footpath link ◄ ● Milford △

● Marquis Drive

● Castle Ring △
△
△ △

● Lichfield △
△

● Weeford

Lower Slaughter

Drayton Bassett ●

Kingsbury △
△

	miles	kms	Total miles
Milford			
Marquis Drive	5.0	8.5	5.0
Castle Ring	4.0	6.5	9.0
Lichfield	6.0	10.0	15.0
Weeford	5.0	8.0	20.0
Drayton Bassett	5.0	8.0	25.0
Kingsbury	4.5	7.5	29.5
Shustoke	6.5	10.5	36.0
Meriden	7.5	12.0	43.5
Berkswell	2.5	4.0	46.0
Balsall Common	2.5	4.0	48.5
Chadwick End	3.5	6.0	52.0

△ ● Shustoke

△

Meriden △ ●

△ Berkswell ●

△ Balsall Common ●

△ Chadwick End ● ◄ Baddesley Clinton

(15)

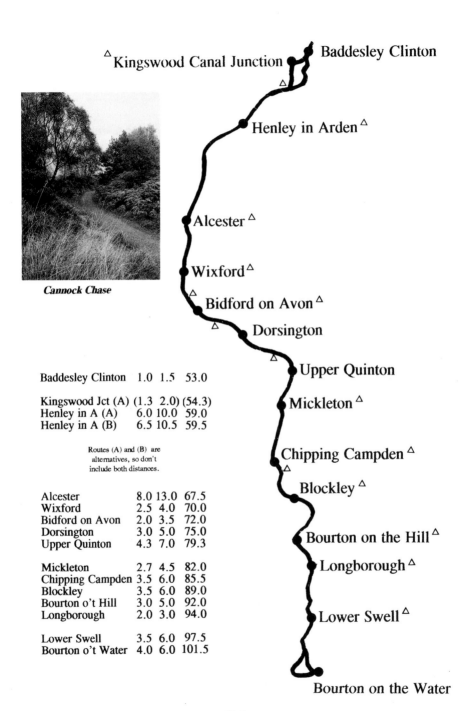

^ΔKingswood Canal Junction Baddesley Clinton

Henley in Arden ^Δ

Alcester ^Δ

Wixford^Δ

Bidford on Avon ^Δ

Dorsington

Cannock Chase

Upper Quinton

Mickleton ^Δ

Chipping Campden ^Δ

Blockley ^Δ

Bourton on the Hill ^Δ

Longborough ^Δ

Lower Swell ^Δ

Bourton on the Water

Baddesley Clinton	1.0	1.5	53.0
Kingswood Jct (A)	(1.3	2.0)	(54.3)
Henley in A (A)	6.0	10.0	59.0
Henley in A (B)	6.5	10.5	59.5

Routes (A) and (B) are
alternatives, so don't
include both distances.

Alcester	8.0	13.0	67.5
Wixford	2.5	4.0	70.0
Bidford on Avon	2.0	3.5	72.0
Dorsington	3.0	5.0	75.0
Upper Quinton	4.3	7.0	79.3

Mickleton	2.7	4.5	82.0
Chipping Campden	3.5	6.0	85.5
Blockley	3.5	6.0	89.0
Bourton o't Hill	3.0	5.0	92.0
Longborough	2.0	3.0	94.0

Lower Swell	3.5	6.0	97.5
Bourton o't Water	4.0	6.0	101.5

(16)

Starting Points and Pubs

Plan your start and finishing points from the map, then refer to this list for details. For each place I have given the map reference, a description of the exact point that it refers to (eg the church), the numbers of the paragraphs in the directions both southbound and northbound and a list of facilities. Some points have no facilities or transport connections but might be useful for picking up or setting down.

If there is a bus service, the word "buses" is followed by a letter indicating the County Council's phone number for enquiries:

> s - Staffordshire 01785 223344
> w - Warwickshire 01926 410410
> m - West Midlands 0121 200 2700
> g - Gloucestershire 01452 425543

The directions start afresh at the listed points to cater for people starting there. To walkers just passing through these places the wording may seem odd or superfluous, but it will still be clear and do you no harm.

Milford (SJ 973212) Para (S1) Tourist Information Office on side road near A513. Pub, shops, cafes, buses(s), car park. *See Transport etc section for footpath link to Stafford.*

Marquis Drive Visitor Centre (SK 005153) (S15X) (N281X) about 1.5 miles north of Hednesford, near Cannock. WC's, refreshments, exhibition, car park.

Castle Ring (SK 045126) Para (S21) (N277) Iron Age fort on S tip of Cannock Chase. Pub, car park. Buses(s) at Gentleshaw 1 mile S (S23)(N274)

(Pub) The Drill Inn (Ansell's), Boney Hay.

(Pub) The Nelson Inn (Greenall's), Cresswell Green

Lichfield (SK 118095) Para (S37) (N261) Cathedral Close. Pubs, shops, tea shops etc, buses(s), trains, pay car parks.

(Pub) Horse & Jockey (Ansells), A51.

Weeford (SK 149039) Para (S45) (N253) Bucks Head Farm on A5. No facilities. Layby park 300 yds E.

Drayton Bassett (SK 193002) Para (S56) (NA239/ NB239) Church. Buses(s), car space.

Kingsbury (SP 216964) Para (S63) (N231) Bus shelter behind White Swan pub. Pubs, shops, buses(m), car space. *Centenary Way.*

(Pub) The Swan (Free House), Whitacre Heath.

Shustoke (SP 237909) (S81) (N211) HoEW crosses A4114 .75 mile E of village. Verge parking.

Meriden (SP 252820) Para (S107) (N181) Queens Head off B4102. Shops, buses(m), car space in village half a mile west.

Berkswell (SP 244791) Para (S114) (N173) A well in front of the church gate. Pubs, shops, buses(m), some car space.

Balsall Common (SP 223771) Para (S120) (N166) Lane meets road by Saracens Head Inn, Buses(m), car space.

Chadwick End (SP 207730) Para (S133) (N150) Orange Tree pub on A4141. Buses(m), some car space.

Baddesley Clinton Manor (SP 200717) Para (SA136/SB136) (N147) Where drive to Manor splits in two. Restaurant (NT), pay car park. *Midland Link.*

Kingswood Canal Junction (SP 186710) Para (SA141) (NA140) Finger post at canal junction. Buses (w), trains at Lapworth station Pub, news & general store, off licence, car park. *Midland Link.*

(Pub) Fleur de Lys (Free House), Lowsonford.

Henley in Arden (SP 151660) Para (S155) (N127) White Swan on main street (A3400). Pubs, shops, tea shops etc, buses(m), trains, parking space.

Alcester (SP 091574) Para (S180) (N103) HoEW's commemorative seat in corner of main square. Pubs, shops, tea shops etc, buses(w), car parks.

Wixford (SP 088545) Para (S185) (N99) Fish Inn on A435 by River Arrow. Limited car space nearby.

(Pub) Broom Tavern (Free House), Broom.

Bidford on Avon (SP 099518) Para (S193) (N90) bridge. Pubs, shops, cafes etc, buses(w), car parks.

(Pub) Cottage of Content (Free House), Barton.

Dorsington (SP 135498) Para (S201) (N83) Green beside church. No facilities, limited car space.

(Pub) Mason's Arms (Free House), Long Marston.

Upper Quinton (SP 178462) Para (S212) (N70) The green. No facilities. *Centenary Way*

Mickleton (SP 162435) Para (S220) (N62) Butcher's shop on main street. Pub and shops, buses(g) limited car space.

Chipping Campden (SP 395153) Para (S230) (N51) Town Hall in High Street. Pubs, shops, tea shops etc, buses(g), car space. *Cotswold Way*

(Pub) Baker's Arms (Free House), Broad Campden.

Blockley (SP163349) Para (S245) (N39) Village Centre. Pubs, shops, cafe, buses(g), limited car space.

Bourton on the Hill (SP 176325) Para (S255) (N32) Bus shelter in village on A44, 2 miles E of Moreton in Marsh. Pub, buses(g), bus & train links at Moreton. No car space.

Longborough (S179293) Para (S260) (N25) War Memorial. Pub, shop, buses(g), car space.

Lower Swell (SP 174255) Para (S272) (N14) War Memorial in village on B4068 1 mile W of Stow on the Wold. Tea shop, pubs, buses(g), limited parking space.

Bourton on the Water (SP 169209) Para (N1) War Memorial in village by A429 Stow on the Wold to Cirencester road. Pubs, shops, tea shops etc, buses(g), car parks. *Oxfordshire Way*

Kingsbury Water Park

Rowington Churchyard

Kinwalsey

(21)

The Heart of England Way

Main Map Symbols

Starting Point	●
Path	·····,····.
Track	----_/⌐
Road/lane	⟨
Railway	+++++++
Canal	⌐_⌐_⌐
Stream/river/lake	
Woodland	
Hedge/fence	
Church	+
Building	◥
Pub	△

Maps are drawn to an approximate
scale of 2.5 ins/1 mile 4cms/1km

Milford

(S1) Start from Tourist Information Centre (on side road). Look R towards Chase & head for white path rising from car park.

(S2) Follow path to pines on CREST. Go ahead & pass pond on your L, then curve L & join track.

(S3) Follow track over crest & go down to crosstracks.

(S4) Follow deep cutting (parallel path on R bank is nicer) to crosstracks by pools.

(S5) Go ahead up banked rising track .75 mile to crosstracks.

(S6) Take track opposite 250yds, round R bend & fork R.

(S7) Pass next R fork & go down valley & up. Cross a track, pass track L, & bend R to meet track on corner (Staffs Way).

(S8) Go ahead on ridge .25 mile to track junction & trig point. [To see glacial boulder go R past trig point.]

(S9) Take L fork (post 4) to next fork (post 5). Go R to crosstracks, then R to car park.

(S10) Go R to entrance, then L a few paces & take rising track. Follow .75 mile to road & cafe.

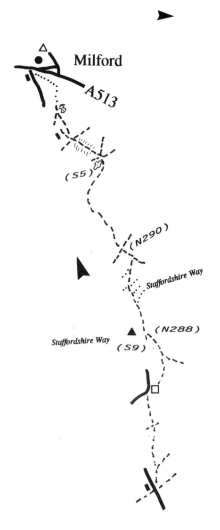

(23)

(N285) DON'T CROSS, take path R parallel with road. Pass track R & go on .6 mile to lane.

(N286) Enter car park & go to far end. Take rising track L to crossways. Go L & join track from R to trig point L & Staffs Way sign. [To see glacial boulder go L past trig point.]

(N287) Follow ridge track past falling track R (Staffs Way), then bend R & take wide track L. ◢

(N288) Cross a track, go ◢ down valley & up to path junction. Go ahead & at next path junction bend L. Follow track 250yds to crossways.

(N289) Take track opposite .75 mile down to cross-tracks. Follow deep cutting (parallel path on L bank is better) down to crossways.

(N290) Bear R, take rising track over crest & bend L. Pass pool on your R, go up between pines & over crest to

Milford

South Lodge, Shugborough

From Castle Ring

Mere Pools

The little village of Milford on the northern tip of Cannock Chase has a pub, a couple of snack bars, a garage, a shop, a Tourist Information Centre and a public loo, which accounts for virtually all the buildings. The reason for all this public provision is two nearby attractions.

Shugborough Hall about a mile to the north-east was first built in 1693, remodelled twice in the next century and is now the home of Lord Lichfield (of Photography) and the County Museum. It is a massive, domineering building fronted by a portico supported on eight gigantic columns. Architectural experts speak well of it. I find the house lumpy and disappointing, but the garden furnishings and follies are dottily delightful. Here is a tiny Greek Doric Temple, a cast iron Chinese bridge, a Lantern of Diogenes, an Arch of Hadrian, a Temple of the Winds and a dramatic railway tunnel. If you are too mean to pay or haven't got the time, go and see the two pretty stone lodges and the fine gates.

The Chase is a steep sided plateau of gravel and sand covering 26 square miles. It rises clear from the rolling green fields of Staffordshire but is cut in two by the steep valley between Rugeley and Cannock. Plant nutrients are quickly washed out of the loose, free draining ground. This is obvious on the open heath in the north-west which is clad with heather, bracken, bilberry and birch. You may find the Cannock Chase berry, a unique local hybrid of cowberry and crowberry. Birds include the hen harrier and nightjar.

Some two thirds of the Chase is dark with Scots and Corsican pines and worked by the Forestry Commission. The young trees are close planted to get rid of side branches and grow knot free timber, so they exclude light. The needles are slow to break down and so form a barren, acid matt. However the pines do attract some birds - crossbill, goldcrest, coal tits, tawney and long eared owls and a rare raptor, the hobby.

The thin acid soil has never been farmed and the Chase was
a dense oakwood until 1550. By 1600 ruthless exploitation
for charcoal to smelt local iron had reduced it to a fraction,
and later sheep grazing encouraged erosion.

From Milford you first climb a little hill crowned with
two gnarled Scots Pine, aged survivors of trees planted on
several hilltops in 1770. Admiral Anson sailed round the
globe in 1740, and since his family lived at Shugborough
and owned the Chase they planted them as a commemor-
ation. Nearby you can see a young plantation of the same
trees which Staffordshire County Council have planted as
successors.

Soon you enter a deep sandy cutting which runs uphill
and dead straight for a quarter mile to Mere Pools. From
here, though paths and tracks run in all directions, there
is no mistaking your route, an embankment sweeps steadily
up the western side of the Chase to the top. This is the
trackbed of the "Tackeroo Railway" built by the Army in
1915 to supply two First World War training camps on the
Chase. It ran from the main line at Milford to the Cannock -
Rugely line at Hednesford.

The trackbed levels out as you reach the top of the Chase
plateau at Coppice Hill, and soon you leave it to follow
peaty paths through heather to the Boulderstone. This huge
piece of granite was carried from the Grampian Mountains
in Scotland in the last ice age.

From this ridge, look out over the sweep of the open Chase,
small round hills rising and falling, and you can see how it
was made. 10,000 years ago the colossal bank of ice that had
covered the Midlands melted, and all the stones, gravel and
sand gouged up across Wales, Scotland and northern England
wwere dumped in heaps, like lorry loads in a builders yard.
Wind, rain and time rounded the contours, new streams
deepened the valleys, and scrub, then trees covered the
slopes.

(S11) Take track opposite cafe .6 mile to cross brook.

(S12) Follow track into forest .3 miles (past 1st track R) & take 2nd track R to road.

(S13) Take track opposite to meet track. Go R 30 paces then L up to next track.

(S14) Go R 30 paces & take track L to crossroads.

(S15) Take road opposite then L fork (Marquis Drive).

Marquis Drive

[TO VISIT centre follow drive R.]

[(S15X) IF STARTING there go to car park entrance, face Centre, go L to road & turn R.]

(S16) Follow road (becomes track) 1.5 miles to A460.

(S17) Cross & take main track 1 mile to crossroads

(S18) Go R 50yds & take 1st track L. Take 1st path R, angling towards road, then L .5 mile, to cross valley bottom.

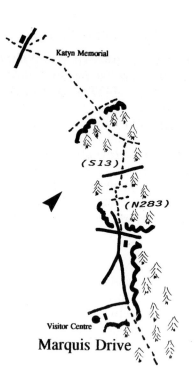

Katyn Memorial

(S13)

(N283)

Visitor Centre

Marquis Drive

(S19) Go up on R fork to road. Go R & round L bend. When track bends R, continue UP.

(S20) AFTER 500yds HoEW takes path L. IF marked & clear, follow - IF NOT;

Go up to where TRACK LEVELS & FARM IN SIGHT AHEAD. Take track L 75 paces (no less), then path R to car park.

Castle Ring

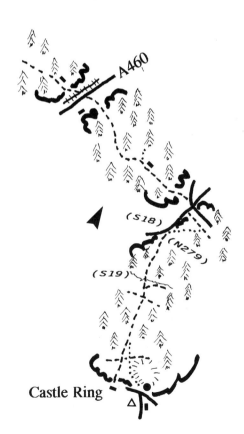

Castle Ring

(N276) From car park enter Ring area & bear L round rampart. Follow path down, cross a path & curve L to join track.

(N277) Go down (crossing track) to start of R bend. Take track L & cross stream. Go .5 mile to near road. ◀

(N278) Take path R & meet track. Go L to road, then R 50yds to junction. ◀

(N279) Take TRACK L at end of Stile Cop Road & follow 1 mile to A460.

(N280) Cross road & railway & follow track 1.5 mile to gates & field L.

Marquis Drive

[TO VISIT Centre follow drive L.]

[(N280X) IF STARTING here - go to park entrance, face Centre & go L to road. Turn L.]

(N281) Continue on road to join road from L & approach crossroads. Bear R onto verge, cross road & take path opposite.

(N282) Follow to meet track. Go R 30 paces, then L to meet track; go R 30 paces, then L to road.

(N283) Take track opposite down to meet forest road.

(N284) Go L 1 mile (out of trees, across brook & rising) to road with cafe opposite. ◀

Near the Boulderstone the HoEW shares a track for a few hundred yards with the Staffordshire Way. To the east is the open Chase and to the west and south it is the same landscape of heather, grass and bracken, but colonized and dominated by birch. It is a beautiful tree, but here has the status of a weed which is invading wide areas.

The Way follows wide, stony tracks along the ridge then bears away to a car park. The chunk of concrete nearby it was once part of a structure for unloading Army coal. Crossing the dome of Ansons Bank, you can use the topo-scope to identify landmarks, if your eyesight is as good as those hen harriers and hobbys. But you don't find Evostick topographs everywhere. Touching a road with a handy cafe, the Way joins a direct, stony track which falls gently to the middle of the Chase. This is the valley of the Sher Brook which rises a few yards to the north.

Beside the track is the Katyn Memorial to 14,000 Polish officers and professionals murdered in the Katyn Forests in 1940. The atrocity was blamed on the Nazis but it has recently emerged that the Russians were responsible.

Crossing the Sher Brook the Way enters conifer woodland. This southern area of the Chase is dominated by Scots and Corsican Pines. The Scots are a native tree, and the edges of plantations have been prettily softened with beech, but the usual complaints about conifers still come to mind.

After a woodland walk you come to Marquis Drive and the Visitor Centre. This large clearing is another link between war and the Chase. By 1938 the Great War camps had gone, sewers choked, hut bases and roads under conifers. The RAF found it cheaper to build a new camp here, which in time had 800 staff and 4,000 trainees. Many aircraft technicians will remember RAF Hednesford, particularly Kitbag Hill, which you will soon follow.

The Way now follows a long straight track down to the deep valley of the Rising Brook, the A460 Rugeley - Cannock road, and the railway. Here 81,000 aircraftmen alighted at a halt and had to carry kitbags up the long hill to the camp. Sandy tracks in a deep, narrow valley take you past the old Youth Hostel to Wandon. The last section of the Chase follows tracks through the woodland of Beaudesert with a final climb to the Iron Age Fort of Castle Ring.

At 801 feet, this is the highest point on the Chase and the HoEW. The ramparts enclose 17 acres which must have been easy to defend because attackers could be seen for miles. For many years you could not see anything because the Forestry Commission had blocked the view with Scots Pine. However that crop has gone and I believe that the open view will now be preserved.

A quiet lane leads from Castle Ring and you pass a grassy hilltop reservoirs to reach Gentleshaw. The curious brick church has a tiny castellated tower and a dark Victorian interior lit by a colourful east window. Nearby, the hulk of a windmill is a beer advert in a pub garden. Both look out over Gentleshaw Common, and although its gorse and grass are different from the Chase you realise that this is an extension of the heathland.

This is an SSSI important for its heathers, grasses and bog plants. There are lizards, skylarks and the green hairstreak butterfly. However bracken is tending to smother the bilberry and heather, and birch and oak have colonized. To preserve the heathland, bracken and trees are cut and heather mown to stimulate new growth. This mimics the farming systems which created the heath; grazing, with cutting of bracken for animal bedding and scrub for fuel.

As you cross the Common and the ground falls away, you see to the south-west a vast industrial landscape. It will soon be out of sight and you will walk green tracks and cross fields. But it tells you that the HoEW runs through the Midlands where millions of people live and work.

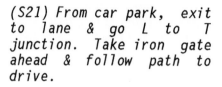 **Castle Ring**

(S21) From car park, exit to lane & go L to T junction. Take iron gate ahead & follow path to drive.

(S22) Go R to L bend. Take path R thro trees to lane. Cross & go ahead 100yds past church L, to topless windmill.

(S23) Take path onto common & follow track parallel with lane 1 mile to cross roads.

(S24) Go R a few paces & cross stile L. Follow R hedge via 2 stiles, then go ahead to cross stream & next stile.

(S25) Go L with hedge to gate & lane. Go L & pass pub to T junction.

(S26) Take track opposite 6 mile to lane. Go ahead, pass pub & fork R for a few paces to next junction.

(S27) Cross lane then plank bridge. Bear L & cross stile. Follow R hedge via 2 stiles, then go ahead to corner gate & lane. ►

(N268) Go ahead & join L hedge. Follow (via 3 stiles) to lane.

(N269) Take lane opposite, curve L past pub & take track L .6 mile to lane.

(N270) Take lane opposite. Pass pub & go on 100yds to cross brook & take gate R.

(N271) Follow R hedge nearly to corner, then cross stile R & brook.

(N272) Go up & cross stile, then with hedge on your R (via 2 stiles) to lane.

(N273) Go R to crossroads. Go L on paths parallel with road 1 mile. Pass old mill to church & join lane.

(N274) Go ahead to road junction with shop L. Take path ahead thro oaks to drive.

(N275) Go L to house & take path L to lane. Take lane opposite .3 mile to car park R.

◄ Castle Ring

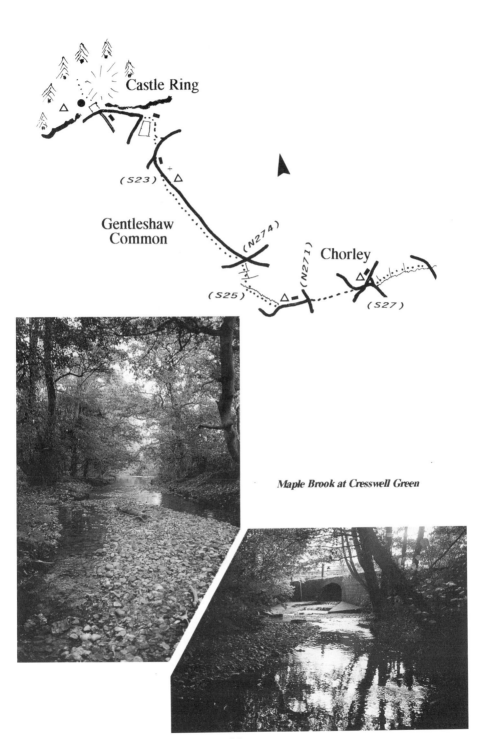

Castle Ring

(S23)

Gentleshaw
Common

(N274)

Chorley

(N271)

(S25)

(S27)

Maple Brook at Cresswell Green

(32)

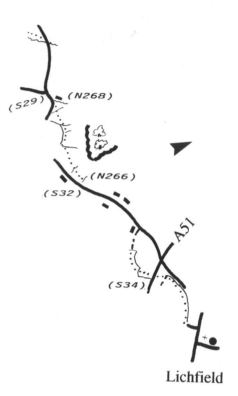

(S28) Go R .3 mile, past lane R, to bend & house L.

(S29) Climb bank L & cross stile. Go half R & cross midfence stile, then keep same line to cross bottom stile.

(S30) Cross stile & bear L to take gate/stile at field corner. Go R on field edge & cross stile.

(S31) **SIGHT wood L & farm R** & head between. Cross stile 50yds L of R field corner. Cross to power pole, stile & lane.

(S32) Go L .6 mile, past Darwin Park, to white lodge R. Pass drive & take track R.

(S33) Cross stile & follow field path along L hedge. Cross stream, & go round L to take stile. Go ahead to stile & A51.

(S34) Cross stile opposite then on to cross next stile. Cross path & follow L fence/hedge round park edge to car park.

Lichfield

(S35) Go thro & continue close to park edge to next car park.

(S36) Go L to road. Go R 175 yds, then L to west front of cathedral.

Lichfield

(33)

West Door

 **Lichfield**

(N260) From cathedral's west front, take street opposite to road, Go R 175 yds & take Shaw Lane L.

(N261) Curve R to car park & continue R bend thro walled passage to park. Go parallel with R wall/fence etc through 2nd car park & round golf course to meet path.

(N262) Take stile opposite & go on to cross next stile to A51. Take stile opposite & go ahead parallel with trees L, to cross stile.

(N263) Follow field path & bear R with hedge to cross bridge. Go on with hedge & take stile & path to lane.

(N264) Go L .6 mile (past The Abnalls & Green End) & take 1st stile R by power pole.

(N265) Cross field & take stile in opposite hedge. Turn half R, pass distant wood R & draw nearer to fence/hedge R, to cross stile.

(N266) Follow line of L hedge & take gate/stile L. SIGHT COTTAGE UP AHEAD & make for it (via stiles), then cross corner stile to lane.

(N267) Go ahead .3 mile (via R bend, past lane L & cottage R) then cross BROOK, & take gates L.

(34)

From Gentleshaw Common on a clear day you can see the
three spires of Lichfield Cathedral. The Way falls gently
towards it on field paths, green tracks and a few connecting
lanes. This is pleasant but unremarkable countryside, though
estate agents would say it has the benefit of two pubs.

After taking a lane down a steep sided holloway you meet a
white lodge with decorative wrought ironwork round the eaves.
The remaining paths to Lichfield are quite level, and if you
must run a Long Distance Footpath into a town, do it this
way, beside the golf course and through the park.

The City of Lichfield astonishes visitors to the area. Here
is a compact and gracious town with fine buildings, a big
park, a beautiful lake by the Cathedral, museums and a
relaxed atmosphere. Annually there is Shrovetide Fair, St
George's Court which appoints officers of the Manor, the
Court of Arraye to review the local militia, Greenhill Bower
which is a procession and crowning of a Bower Queen, the
Lichfield Festival of music, drama and poetry, Dr Johnsons'
Birthday celebrations and the Sheriff's Ride around the City
boundaries. But in spite of all this, with even the Tourist
Information Office an early 18th century gem, Lichfield
is quiet and almost off the tourist trail.

But Lichfield has its Cathedral. The Cathedral Close is
an intimate square of sanely reasonable Georgian and
Victorian buildings in stucco or mellow Midlands brick.
Soaring above are the three spires, a design unique in
Britain and built of brown sandstone in the Early English
and Decorated styles. The Cathedral suffered some terrible
damage in 1541 during Henry VIII's Reformation and later
in the Civil War.

Almost nothing remains from the Norman period, the
transepts are early 13th century, the nave a little later,
with the west front and east ends edging into the next
century. However the building was so extensively

remodelled between 1856 and 1890 by Sir Giles Gilbert
Scott that the detail is mainly his. You are looking at
what has become a Victorian Cathedral with all the
virtues and vices that implies.

The richly encrusted west front dominates the building and
the Close, a job creation scheme for masons with niches,
crockets, pinnacles, arcading, tracery and three rows of
statues. Kings, saints and for all I know, an early football
team examine visitors - pensive, determined, noble, pious,
downcast or plain bored. They share a profound gloom
and only King Offa seems to be attempting a protest - have
we got to be like this? Pevsner opines that the west front is
not wholly satisfactory and the spires do not aspire enough.

Some people may respond more to the modest, domestic
buildings of the Close, their simplicity and restrained
proportions. But whatever you think of the outside, the
interior of Lichfield Cathedral is exciting, with the later
additions High Victorian at its best. There are awesome
fountains of stone, richly coloured windows, intricate tiles
and a splendid screen. Get a guide book and have a look.

Dr Samuel Johnson was born in 1709 in the house on the
corner of the Market Square and Breadmarket Street. As
journalist, essayist and poet, he complied the first English
dictionary and became a major literary figure, treasured for
his wit and wisdom. He is commemorated in the Birthplace
Museum and a surprisingly youthful statue. Nearby is a fine
bronze of his friend and biographer, Boswell.

It is quite a long way, out over the railway, through the
suburbs and along the A51. But it is the only urban section
of the Way and the streets and gardens are pleasant enough.
From the Horse & Jockey on the A51 there is a two and a
half mile straight over the sandy dome of Packington Moor.
In spite of being farmed, it is wild and quiet and feels open
and high, though barely 40 feet above Lichfield. Imagine it
unfarmed, with gorse and heather, and you realise that it
was once heath like the Chase.

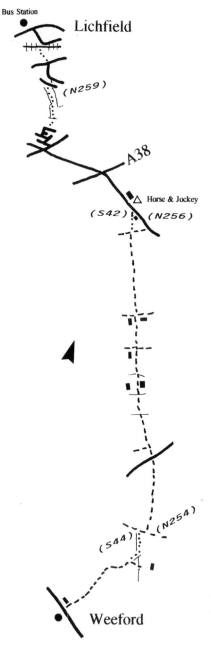

Lichfield

(S37) From west front of cathedral, go to far end of close & turn R. Brass waymark discs let into pavements lead you across city centre to bus station facing Birmingham Road.

(S38) Cross Birmingham Rd. Go L past Ambulance Station drive, then R on next street.

(S39) Follow street to end & cross railway. Follow path to road. Take Oakhurst opposite to No 45, & take fenced path R.

(S40) Follow tarmac path to road. Cross & go on with wall on your L. Cross open section & enter fenced path to road.

(S41) Go R & follow road (via bends) to T junction. Go L to T junction with hedged lane, then R to A51

(S42) Go L .75 mile. Pass Horse & Jockey & take path R opposite post box. ►

Weeford

(N252) Enter Bucks Head Farm & follow track. Take R bend then L bend, & at next R bend by gateway, (with house 150yds R) leave track.

(N253) Go with hedge on your R & take gate. Go L to gate & track. Go R 25 yds & take gateway L.

(N254) Follow fenced track between fences & KEEP SAME LINE for 2.5 miles;
- cross lane
- track becomes wooded path to field
- pass oak on your R
- pass farm L & house R
- pass farm L
- go thro farm
- track to T junction
- follow field edge &
via gate to A51

(N255) Go L .75 mile to Quarry Hills Lane R.

(N256) Take QH Lane, then 1st L (Borrowcop), then 1st R (Hillside). Go R, round top bend & take path L by lampost.

(N257) Follow tarmac path, cross open area, then with wall on your R to road. ◀

(N258) Take path by "cattle grid" to road; go L to road. Cross, take path behind railings & cross railway to road. Go L a few paces then R to main road.

(N259) Cross & go L to bus station. Brass waymark discs let in pavements guide you across city centre to cathedral.

◀ Lichfield

S

(S43) Keep SAME LINE 2.5 miles via gates & stiles,
- rise over crest & pass between buildings
- pass farm R
- pass between farms R & L
- join hedged path
- cross track then lane
to T junction of tracks.

(S44) Go R 20 yds & take gate L. Follow R hedge 200 yds & take 1st gate R. Follow L hedge & join track. Go ahead & follow to A5.

Weeford

(S45) At farm gate face A5 & go R 100 yds. Take lane L, cross bridge, & cross stile ahead.

(S46) Follow L hedge & cross stile. **Sight conifers ahead/L & lone tree beyond.** Head for lone tree (if path obstructed follow L field edge) & cross stile.

(S47) Head up middle of valley (via gateway) to crest 100yds L of trees R. Cross stile & follow R fence down to track. Go L thro farm to lane.

(S48) Go R .6 mile (past farm R, houses L & 2 stiles L) to gateway L. Go on 100yds to enter hedge gap L (opposite power pole R).

(S49) **SIGHT BIG TREE CLUMP** ahead & slightly R, then head for lone oak on its L. When its in view, go down to cross midhedge stile.

(S50) Bear L to power pole. Join field track & go thro farm to lane.

(N244) Take track thro farm, bear R thro gate & follow grass track to end.

(N245) Go to top L field corner & cross stile. Bear L up rise & (when in view) sight distant farm. Head just R of it to hedge gap & lane.

(N246) Go R .6 mile (past houses R & 1st farm L) to 2nd farm L.

(N247) Go L through farm to 2nd gate. DON'T TAKE IT. Go up R by hedge & cross stile.

(N248) Go over crest & down middle of valley (via gate), to corner of wood R. Cross stile.

(N249) Go R round field edge. Look ahead to see projecting hedge corner & head for STILE just L.

(N250) Cross stile & follow R hedge to stile & track. Go ahead to A5.

(N251) Go R 100yds to Bucks Head Farm at

◄ **Weeford**

(39)

Route (A) on pages (41) and (42) was the original & intended line of the Way. It follows pleasant field paths on established Rights of Way but for a short lane into Drayton Bassett. Route (B) uses 2.5 miles of road.

The lane part of Route (A) is not a public road but people have walked it for years. The Parish Council has claimed that it should be shown on maps as a Right of Way, and the case has been making slow progress up the County Council's list of similar claims. At the time of writing Route (A) is not officially available to us. Phone me on 01926 776363 to check the current position.

NEXT

SOUTHBOUND page (41)
NORTHBOUND page (42)

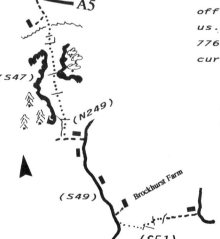

Route (A)

(SA51) Take gate opposite & go up between hedges. Go parallel with R hedge past power pole with small brother, & via gateway to cross stile.

(SA52) Follow R hedge via 2 fields & cross stile. Cross field diagonally to L of house. Take stile & path to A453.

(SA53) Go L & cross to Hill Farm. Follow drive & fork to end of stone wall. Go L thro farm & take small gate, then stile ahead.

(SA54) Follow L hedge & pass pond. Go round field corner & on 100yds to tree, then go L thro hedge gap. ◀

(SA55) **SIGHT FARM AHEAD**, head for L end of buildings & join track. Go thro farm & follow lane to village.

next para (S56) ▶

****

Route (B)

(SB51) Follow lane R .5 mile past L fork, to A453.

(SB52) Go L 300 yds & take lane R. Go 2 miles (past 3 lanes R) to village

next para (S56) ▶

Drayton Bassett

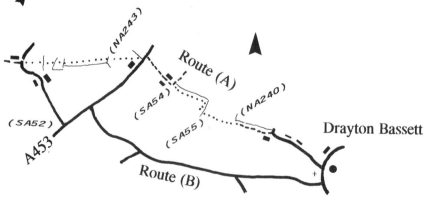

(41)

Drayton Swing Bridge

have you read the note on page (40)?

Drayton Bassett

 ### Route (A)

(NA239) From church pass Post Office to take lane L. Go thro farm & follow field track to end of R hedge.

(NA240) Keep same line midfield to R side of tree clump & cross hedge gap. Go R with hedge (round field corner) to stile & track.

(NA241) Go ahead thro farm to end, then bear R to A453.

(NA242) Cross road & go L 50 yds to take stile on R of house. Follow fenced path to field. Cross diagonally & take far corner stile. ◀

(NA243) Follow L hedge (via 2 fields) & cross stile. Keep same line via gateway, & power pole with small brother. Head for far end of house ahead & take gate to lane.

next - para (N244) ◀

****

Route (B)

(NB239) Face church & go L. Follow lane 2 miles (past 3 lanes L) to A453.

(NB240) Go L 300yds & take lane R. Follow .5 mile (past farm (1). Go L at fork to farm (2) (Hints Farm) on R bend.

next - para (N244) ◀

Drayton Bassett

(S56) Face church & go R on lane to A4091. Cross road then canal. Walk with canal on your R 2.5 miles to Curdworth Bottom Lock.

(S57) Just before houses take track L. Curve R, go 350yds past lakes L, then turn L.

(S58) Go parallel with lake L to its end by house R.

(S59) Take path R, & at fork go R to T junction. Go L under M42 plus 150yds to junction with path R.

For excursion via Visitor Centre see page (48).

(S60) From junction with path follow hard track to T junction with car park R. Go L 22 paces into field.

(S61) Go R by trees through 2 fields & go half R to brick bridge.

(S62) Cross River Tame & follow path past church. Follow track to road & bus shelter R.

Kingsbury

Kingsbury

(N231) From bus shelter behind White Swan, take track to church. Pass it on your L, go down steps & cross river.

For excursion via Visitor Centre see page 48.

(N232) From end of brick bridge go half R to opposite field corner. Follow edge of trees to playground.

(N233) Go L 22 paces & take hard track R to meet path L by finger post.

(N234) At finger post, put your back to side path & go L. Pass under M42, plus 150yds to junction.

(N235) Go R to next fork. Go L to R bend by house L.

(N236) Go ahead with lake on your R to its corner. Go R & follow path past lakes & houses to canal.

(N237) Go R 2.5 miles to battlemented footbridge.

(N238) Cross canal & A4091. Take lane opposite .5 mile to village green.

Drayton Bassett

NEXT see note page (40)

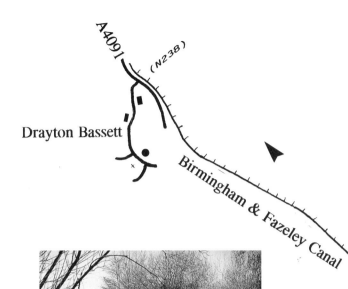

A4091

(N238)

Drayton Bassett

Birmingham & Fazeley Canal

(N237)

(S57)

Map of
Water Park to
Kingsbury
on page 47

Kinsgbury Water Park

The Causeway and Kingsbury Church

(44)

There is a village at Weeford, but this is not it. The HoEW meets the A5 and there is nothing to be seen but Bucks Head Farm, not unattractive, and rushing traffic, which is. When I wrote the fourth edition of this guide I am sure there were fallow deer antlers over the farm's front door, but it seems to have shed them. Perhaps the lintel is growing some more. No one can love this A5 which it is not even an easy drive, but it is still an exciting idea with a rich history. The road was first engineered by the Romans who built a camp nearby at Wall, and rebuilt by Thomas Telford in 1815. In one direction it runs to London and in the other Hollyhead.

From the A5 the Way runs down a quiet lane and crosses the Black Brook into a totally different type of landscape. After sandy, open heath comes a range of grassy little mountains where you sweep up a green valley to a curving crest topped with conifers.

A quiet lane, hardly more than a track, takes you half a mile south to the turn east at Brockhurst Farm. Since the HoEW was planned this has been successively a pig farm and dog kennels and was later destined to become a golf club. However, the developers collapsed leaving the surrounding fields a moonscape of half dug bunkers and hills of earth. After a period as a ruin it is now a private house.

From the farm there is a very slight climb and fall. It is not immediately obvious, but this is the plain of the River Tame. The landscape flattens, field follows field with grass, barley, root crops and hedgerows as the HoEW heads for Drayton Bassett and the valley bottom.

Drayton Bassett has a church and a shop cum post office but no pub, all due to Robert Peel who bought Drayton Manor and estate in 1790 and became the first Sir Robert. His son became the long serving MP for Tamworth and the Prime Minister who established the police force. The second Sir Robert did not like being stared at or approve of his tenants gossiping by their front doors, so several cottages by the green were built with entrances at the back. The village now has a working men's club to offset its worst privation. The estate and Manor were sold in the 1920's and the grounds are now a zoo.

St Peter's church was built in the 13th century but only the base of the tower survives from this period. The upper part is in the later perpendicular style, the nave is 18th century and the chancel Victorian. There is a seriously gothic monument of 1850 to Sir Robert (PM) Peel.

You join the Birmingham & Fazeley Canal at a dotty little footbridge supported by battlemented brick towers. No one seems to know why. The Canal was authorized by Parliament in 1784 and runs 15 miles from Fazeley Junction near Tamworth to Birmingham, where it joins a maze of road, rail and water links under the whirling arms of Spaghetti Junction. The HoEW follows the towpath south through open farmland to Kingsbury Water Park.

For 50 years gravel was extracted from the floor of the Tame Valley. When the works were abandoned in 1973 they left 600 acres of pits, large and small, separated by narrow necks of land. Some of the pits had been filled with fly ash from a nearby power station but most brimmed naturally with water. Warwickshire County Council took over the site and developed it as rather a special Country Park. They encouraged natural colonisation by mosses, grasses, reeds, willows, brambles, birch and oak, added to it with with new plantings and laid tracks and paths. There are 30 lakes and pools, the largest being the 66 acre Bodymoor Heath Water. Hemlingford Water is only a little smaller. At the Visitor Centre you can see an exhibition with video, pick up leaflets and use the cafe.

The park is a wonderful place for birdwatchers and naturalists, and you can fish, row, sail, windsurf, sink your model boat, ride horses, walk, orienteer, muck about getting wet and muddy or sink exhausted onto the grass.

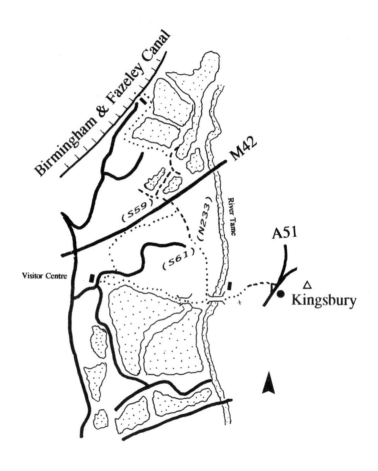

Kingsbury Water Park

(S59A) Take side path .5 mile (at fork go R) to drive.

(S59B) Cross, go R over bridge & curve L to T junction of paths, with Visitor Centre R.

(S59C) Go L to fork then curve L to cross bridge & join track.

(S59D) Go R with lakes on your R 450yds (ignore L fork) & cross L of 2 bridges.

(S59E) Follow causeway to River Tame bridge.

next para (S62) ▶

(N231A) Follow causeway & cross steel bridge. Go ahead on track with lakes on your L 450yds, to fork on corner of lake.

(N231B) Go L across foot-bridge, then fork R to next path R, with Visitor Centre ahead.

(N231C) Go R & curve R to cross bridge. Go on 20 paces & turn L.

(N231D) Cross drive & follow path .5 mile to T junction with finger post.

next para (N234) ◀

⟨S⟩ Kingsbury

(S63) From bus shelter behind White Swan, pass White Swan then Royal Oak & cross A51. Pass No 81 & take path L.

(S64) Follow clear path & cross bridge. Ignore path L & go 200yds to take steps R.

(S65) Follow fenced path (past path R) & cross railway. Keep same line to lane.

(S66) Cross & go ahead to fence. Go R & round corner to range road.

(S67) Cross road by flag pole into field. Go L on field edge UP TO HUTS.

Face them & look up R to see red & white farm on RIDGE, & BIGGEST oak 200yds L.

(S68) Go on to corner flag & L 150yds to start of hedge & sign. Turn half R & head upfield to ridge & biggest oak.

(S69) Join grass track & pass farm to lane. Go ahead to T junction. Go L 100yds & cross stile R.

▶

(N225) Go L & take lane R to farm. Take green track ahead to end by big oak.

(N226) **CARE. Ahead see church then look L to big red brick wall.** Head for wall & (when in view) for L end of field bottom trees.

(N227) Go L to flagpole on corner, then R on field edge to last pole. Cross road & take green track round R bend to field end. Go L to lane.

(N228) Cross & follow field edge to cross railway. Follow fenced path & take steps R.

(N229) Go L with L fence & cross bridge. Go L to A51.

(N230) Cross & go R to pass Royal Oak L. Go L before White Swan to bus shelter.

Kingsbury

NEXT para (N231) page (43)
◀

(S70) Follow R hedge (via stiles) to hedge corner. Turn half L to projecting hedge corner, then with hedge on your R to lane.

(S71) Go R to T junction. Take track ahead .4 mile to field.

(S72) Go half R across field to corner by trees & take small gate.

(S73) Go ahead (via gate) & join track to B4098.

▶

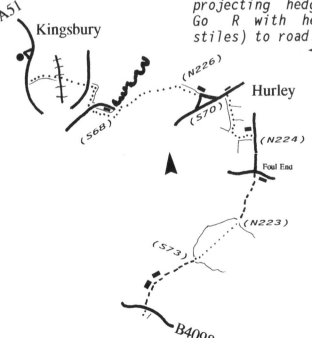

(N221) Take lane opposite. At hairpin bend keep same line & (via 2 kissing gates) reach field corner.

(N222) Look half L to **SIGHT HOUSES** on low hill. Note thick hedge coming down to this field & head for its bottom end & join track.

(N223) Follow .4 mile to lane junction. Go ahead .3 mile to one field before houses L, & take gateway L

(N224) Follow L hedge to corner. Bear R to projecting hedge corner. Go R with hedge (via stiles) to road.

◀

The River Tame has two sources, one near Wolverhampton
and another some 8 miles south at Blackheath. The two streams
meet in the unpromising environment of the M6 near Walsall
and the motorway follows the valley to Spaghetti Junction.

It gurgles on through east Birmingham, collects from the
gigantic Minworth Sewage Works, then turns north towards
Tamworth. In its 47 miles to the Trent the Tame is not a
pretty stream, but the hard working drain of one of the
biggest conurbations in the world. The Environment Agency
feeds it through special lakes at Lea Marston to allow
contaminated sediment to settle. Water quality has improved,
although on the EA's A to F scale the Tame remains mainly
Grade E. Incredibly, a healthy fish population has been
established south of Lea Marston. Anyway, the little brick
bridge and causeway by which you cross the river to Kingsbury village and attractive.

As you cross the Tame you can see Kingsbury Mill, an 18th
century foundry where guns were made during the Napoleonic
Wars. Above is the church of St Peter and St Paul, which has
a Norman nave.A "bury" was a fortified house and this one was
used by King Offa of Mercia whose capital was at Tamworth.
Kingsbury and Hurley further on, were mining villages which
lost their pits.

Leaving Kingsbury you cross the old Midland Railway line
from Birmingham to Burton on Trent and skirt a rifle range.
It is conventional to warn people to be careful when red
flags are flying, but I am not sure what you should do. A
vast rising arable field follows, but as you near the crest
of the ridge at Camp Farm, views open out, and you leave
the Tame Valley for the first time in seven miles.

The HoEW does not enter Hurley, but there are shops and
pubs if you care to wander in for half a mile. Like , Kingsbury it was a workaday mining village, but had its bit of
Civil War history when a canon ball dropped down the
chimney of Atherstone House.

Fields and a lane take you to misnamed Foul End and half a mile of nice green lane. The dominating objects in a fair panorama of fields and woods used to be the three cooling towers of Hams Hall Power Station, now mysteriously vanished. It is not that I mind people making off with these things, but it made rubbish of two route directions and a photograph.

There is another green lane past Halloughton Hall, a continuation of the track from Foul End, then fields and a lane to join a railway. After a delicate, almost pretty, steel railway footbridge there are a few low lying fields, which means that you have briefly re-entered the Tame Valley. But you are soon over a crest and on the long march beside another railway, the Midland Railway's Birmingham to Nuneaton line.

Beyond the trees are the two Shustoke Reservoirs, originally built for Birmingham. The nearby Whitacacre Heath Water Works in gaunt Victorian Gothic might equally be a church, a hospital, a monastery or a University. When the City's Elan Valley water came on stream in about 1905, Shustoke was handed over to supply Nuneaton and Coventry.

Whitacre Heath

(52)

(S74) Take stile opposite.
Go ahead & cross stile.
Head 50 yds R of bottom L
field corner & cross
stile. Go L to stile &
lane.

(S75) Go R to foot of
bridge & take track L.
Round L bend, go .3 mile
to steel bridge R & take
gate.

(S76) Follow L hedge &
cross plank bridge. Bear
L to field corner & cross
twin stiles.

(S77) Go R 25 yds to field
corner. Go L with ditch
on your R, & cross stile.
Cross field diagonally to
stile & lane. ➤

(N215) Bear L & cross lane
to take stile L of house.
Cross field diagonally &
take stile.

(N216) Follow L hedge,
then ditch, to field
corner. Go R to 2 stiles.

(N217) Take L stile & go
parallel with R hedge to
cross stile. Follow R
hedge to field corner &
take gate to railside
track.

(N218) Follow .3 mile &
bend R to lane.

(N219) Go R .4 mile to
lane R. Cross stile
opposite & bear R to take
midfence stile.

(N220) **Put your back to
stile & look half L to
gate & stile on crest.**
Head for them (via
midhedge stile) & reach
B4098. ◄

(S78) Take stile opposite. Follow L fence round to far corner. **Sight trees on crest** & go up midfield to pass L end. Go down field edge & cross railway.

(S79) Go L .9 mile & take gate. Go R, pass house R. When fence bends away R, follow it & cross stile to field.

(S80) Go R a few paces to hedge corner, then R on field edge to meet hedge. Go L up hedge (via stile) to A4114.

Shustoke

Shustoke

(N211) Cross stile on "non cottage" side. Follow L hedge (via stile) to bottom corner. Go R with hedge to its end.

(N212) Go L a few paces & take stile L. Follow L fence, then follow channel & cross bridge to railway.

(N213) Take gate L & follow fenced path .9 mile to 50yds from brick bridge.

(N214) Cross railway & follow L hedge to crest. Go down to L of house, follow fence to stile & lane.

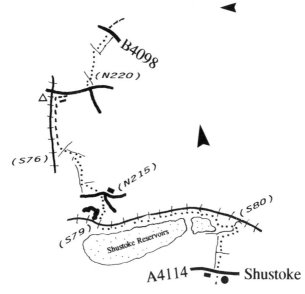

(S81) Take stile on L of cottages & follow R hedge (via 2 stiles) to field corner stile. DO NOT CROSS.

(S82) Go L with hedge on your R & cross stile. Go on 60yds & cross midhedge stile R.

(S83) Follow L hedge (via stile) to corner stile & lane. Go ahead to next corner & take track ahead into field.

(S84) Follow L hedge & cross corner stile. Go ahead & cross midhedge stile. Go ahead to R corner of wood (via stile & bridge). Follow wood to track.

(S85) Cross & pass gateway L. Join L hedge for 25yds to beneath POWER LINES. **SIGHT wooded hill ahead/R and its L slope.** Cross field to where slope meets hedge.

(S86) Go down with hedge on your L to 1st oak. Cross hedge & bear R to pass midfield oak on your L. Meet wood 150 yds L of field corner. ►

(N205) Bear L to pass midfield oak on your R, then curve L to top hedge oak & cross hedge.

(N206) Go up with R hedge to projecting corner. **Turn L & sight red brick shed.** Aim for its near end & join R hedge to track.

(N207) Cross track & take path along R hedge to cross stile. Go ahead & cross stile.

(N208) **Sight church spire & 2 phone poles to its L.** Cross field to between poles & take stile. Bear R past 2 midfield oaks & cross stile. Follow R hedge to lane.

(N209) Go ahead to next corner & cross stile. Follow R hedge via 2 stiles & cross 3rd.

(N210) Go L with hedge (via stile) to next field corner & stile. DO NOT CROSS. Go R with hedge (via 2 stiles) to stile & B4114.

◄ **Shustoke**

(55)

(S87) Cross bridge & follow path to cross twin stiles. Go L, round field corner, & go thro dingle to lane.

(S88) Go R 350yds to T junction. Go L a few paces & enter gateway R.

(S89) **NB woods all round field & gap at far end.** Make for L side of gap & cross stile.

(S90) Follow wood edge & take gate. Cross field diagonally to stile & lane. ▶

(N200) Go diagonally L to corner of L hedge & wood, & take gateway. Follow wood edge & cross stile.

(N201) **Sight 4th pylon from R.** Head for it & exit via field corner gap to lane.

(N202) Go L a few paces to fork, go R 350yds. Just before lane junction take path L.

(N203) Follow to field, go round field corner & cross 2 stiles R.

(N204) Go thro dingle & cross bridge to field.

◀

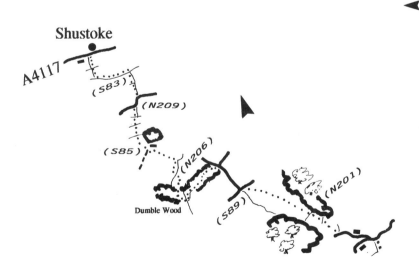

(S91) Go L, pass lane R & drive R, & just after cross stile R.

(S92) Go ahead a few paces to hedge corner, then keep same line across field into hedge gap. Go with hedge on your L (repeat L) & cross stile.

(S93) Bear L across field corner & take stile into copse. Go thro to stile & field.

(S94) Go R on field edge & cross stile. Bear L & cross midhedge stile. Go up midfield & cross stile to lane.

(S95) Take stile opposite. Go up field edge, cross stile & pass farm. Join track to stile & lane.

(S96) Take lane opposite, pass service road L & cross corner stile. Put your back to stile, head for lone ash tree & cross stile. Go to far R corner stile & lane.

►

(N192) Go L a few paces & cross stile R. Cross field diagonally to mid-hedge stile by gate (under lone ash tree).

(N193) Cross stile & head for far end of houses R, to stile & lane. Go R to lane junction.

(N194) Take track opposite, pass farm on your R & cross stile. Go to bottom R field corner & cross stile to lane.

(N195) Take stile opposite & cross midfield to take stile. Bear R to bottom R field corner stile.

(N196) Cross stile & follow L hedge 150 yds to cross stile L. Go thro copse & cross stile.

(N197) Sight power pole on hill ahead & oak on its R - take stile beneath. Follow R hedge to corner.

(N198) Go ahead midfield to recessed field corner & cross stile to lane.

(N199) Go L past drive, lane & farm R, then on 200yds to cross stile R.

◄

(S97) Go L a few paces up to farm gate & take stile in bushes R. Go R & just before double shed, cross stiles & yard.

(S98) Go parallel with L hedge & take gate. Pass hawthorns on your L & cross M6.

(S99) Take stile R & bear L to cross field corner stile. Go up field & cross top midhedge stile.

(S100) Follow L hedge & cross stile. Go ahead & cross stile to B4102.

▶

(N189) Go L to end of farm wall & cross stile R. Go ahead & cross stile. Follow R hedge & cross stile.

(N190) Go to bottom R field corner. Cross stile & bear L to cross M6.

(N191) Go ahead passing hawthorns on your R & take gate. Aim to R side of double sheds (L of farm) & cross 2 stiles. Bear R & cross stile to lane.

◀

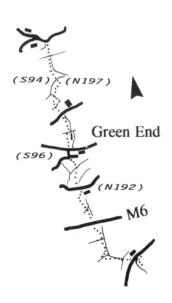

(S94) (N197)

Green End

(S96)

(N192)

M6

Shustoke Reserviors

From Shustoke Reservoirs the Way rises to cross the A4114 and a broad hump of arable farmland. Rerouting of paths in this area enables us to avoid a farm which was attractive but had a memorably floodable yard. Passing some isolated old cottages on the corner of a wood, the path start to fall towards a little valley with a mile long dingle called Dumble Wood.

This is a good point at which to acknowledge the physical work of the Heart of England Way Association. Organised by Brian Keates, the bridge crossing the stream was built by them from ground works to handrail. People pay no particular attention to stiles unless they give cause for complaint. But most of those you cross on the HoEW have at some time been repaired or replaced by this handful of volunteers.

Dumble Wood is first crossed, then entered, when it becomes very pretty. The big trees are all oaks and the understorey coppiced hazel. This is a regime called "coppice with standards" which was once widespread in the Midlands.

It allowed the fast growing, shrubby hazel to be cut back regularly for poles, staves and sticks to make fencing, hurdles and baskets. In the longer term the oaks provided big timbers for ploughs and building materials. Dumble Wood has not been cut in some years and the old management may have been abandoned. Like many old woods, it could become a dark thicket. Butterflies and many woodland plants would disappear because they flourish when there is light on the ground. The county wildlife trusts and the Woodland Trust often use coppice with standards management.

The Way follows a lane to a long arable field with dense woods on either side. Once or twice I have seen fallow deer crossing between them with only heads and antlers visible over the tall barley. The stile into the next field marks a change in the character of the Way. Now you are onto grass, the landscape becomes a little more pastoral, there are more small hills and woods - typical Arden.

Heading south, the fields rise and fall over modest hills into small valleys with tree lined streams. The tiny lanes and farms seem quite remote and the M6 is a nasty shock. Estimate the distance at which you can hear it. This unremitting, brainless roar surely makes the case against motorways.

Happily you are soon across the monster and off up a bank. From here look west towards Birmingham for the first of several amazing views. The ground levels again at a road by Hayes Hall Farm which has fine buildings and a super pond.

The Way continues to climb gently to a summit and a wood called Meriden Shafts. The name arises from past surface mining in shallow pits. None are visible from the right of way and it would be unwise to look for them. Most of the trees are larch and Scots pine, though the larch nearest the footpath has recently been felled to create a light and airy wood which which will attract butterflies and wildflowers.

S

(S101) Go L to farm gate & cross stile opposite. Go R, round field corner, & follow R hedge to wood corner.

(S102) Follow track with wood L 500yds to waymark post. (If you meet hedge go back 80yds.) Go R & cross stile. Go ahead to stile & lane.

(S103) Go L 400yds, (past farm L) to ruin on L bend. Take stile ahead & follow L hedge up to wood. Cross stile onto track.

(S104) Go L 50yds & cross stile R. Follow woodland path & exit at stile.

(S105) Cross plank bridge & go up midfield, bearing L to take hedge gap. Go ahead & cross stile L of sheds. Follow L hedge to stile & lane.

(S106) Go R 1 mile (past lane R, under A45 & past lane R) to Queens Head.

Meriden

(N181) Face Queens Head & take lane on its R (not slip road). Follow .75 mile (past L fork, under A45, past L fork) to caravan park.

(N182) Go on to pass next bungalow & cross stile L. Follow R hedge & cross stile.

(N183) Go down midfield & thro gappy hedge. Bear L to bottom corner & cross plank bridge.

(N184) Cross stile & follow wood path up to stile & track. Go L 50 yds & cross stile R.

(N185) Follow R hedges (via 3 fields) to lane.

(N186) Go L 300yds to sharp L bend, power pole & "Harvest Hill Lane" sign.

(N187) Cross stile R. Go ahead midfield & cross stile & bridge to wood edge track.

(N188) Go L past wood, then follow L hedge to field end & cross stile to lane.

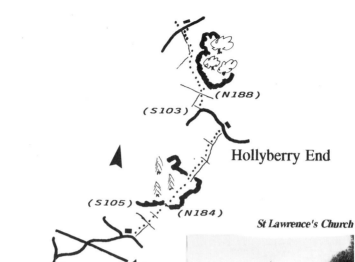

(N188)

(S103)

Hollyberry End

(S105)

(N184)

St Lawrence's Church

A45

Meriden

B4102

Queen's Head

MERIDEN

Village Pond

(62)

⬠S Meriden

(S107) Take steps opposite Queens Head & cross B4102. Take stile, follow L hedge up & pass church to lane.

(S108) Go R, round R bend & pass Old Vicrage L to take 1st field gate L. Follow L hedge down to cross bottom stile.

(S109) Follow L hedges (cross stile, bear L past 2 gates & cross corner stile) then up field edge & cross stile.

(S110) Bear L to top midhedge tree clump & cross stile. Follow L hedge to stile & join track to lane.

(S111) Take gate opposite. Follow L hedge to corner & take gap to next field. Go with hedge on your R, thro hedge gap & on 200yds to pond. Just past it cross hidden stile R.

(S112) Pass pond on your R, head for house & join track. Follow to road.

(S113) Go L 300yds to near houses, cross road & take gate. Go thro wood, follow L hedge (via stiles) & thro churchyard to lane.

Berkswell ⬠N

(N173) From Well take small gate on corner of churchyard. Follow path & take kissing gate. Follow R hedge & go through spinney to road.

(N174) Go L 300yds & take 1st lane R. Pass all houses & cross stile.

(N175) Go L by hedge till it bends L, then keep ahead past pond & cross corner stile. Go L on field edges (via hedge gaps) to gate & lane.

(N176) Take track ahead & pass gate R to cross stile. Follow R hedge & cross stile. Go to bottom L field corner & cross stile.

(N177) Follow R hedge .5 mile via stiles (& past 2 gates R), to take top midhedge gate to lane.

(N178) Go R round church & before white house take small gate L.

(N179) Curve R past church & follow R hedge to B4102.

(N180) Cross & take steps to Queens Head pub.

Berkswell

◄ Meriden

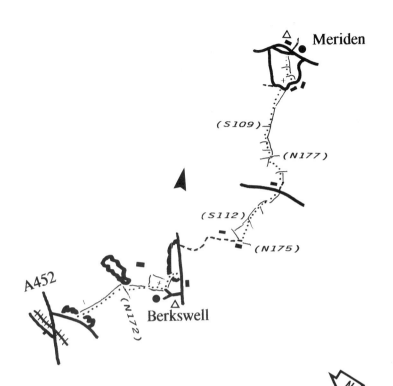

Meriden

(S109)

(N177)

(S112)

(N175)

A452

(N172)

Berkswell

Berkswell

(S114) From Well go to church & pass porch on your R. Bear L & take gate.

(S115) Follow causeway, pass thro wood & take iron gate. Go L 50yds to pass gate on your R, then with fence on your R (via wood) to lane.

(S116) Go R to A452. Cross, go L over railway & take lane R.

N

(N170) Go L 250yds. Cross & take 1st lane R. Follow 300yds to just past 1st gate L, & take kissing gate L.

(N171) Follow wood path, then fence to its end, & go on 100 yds to bridge.

(N172) Take kissing gate R & go thro wood. Follow causeway & take kissing gate. Pass church on your L to gate & lane.

◄ **Berkswell**

Down lanes then to the middle of England at Meriden.
At least, this is what Meriden claims, though Ashby de la
Zouche argues something similar. The Way does not run
through the village but shoots uphill from the Queens
Head pub to the Church of St Lawrence.

Lady Godiva provided the first church in 1147. Norman
portions remain but after many additions and alterations the
present building was largely completed in the 16th century.
The inevitable Victorian extras include the porch, organ
room and vestry. The square tower is 16th century and if
it seems rather squat, it used to support a spire. Now it sits
amongst a scatter of old gravestones, the archetypal English
parish church. However the red sandstone is weathering
badly and the church needs many urgent repairs.

Meriden village is nearly half a mile away. There is a 14th
century market cross to mark the centre of England, a village
pond, a post office, a couple of shops and restaurants and
the big, comfortable Bull's Head. From the early 1900's
Meriden was a magnet for weekend cyclists from Birmingham and Coventry, and they erected the memorial on the
green to those who had died in the two world wars.

But high on the hill by the church is the best place to be in
Meriden. Look out over the village to the horizon. There is
Birmingham, and on a clear day you should be able to pick
out the tall white buildings in the centre, the Telecom
tower, the Rotunda and the lofty flats at Horsefair called
the Sentinels.

It is hard to imagine that the outer suburbs of Coventry and
Birmingham are only some 4 miles each side of Meriden.
Planners call it the Meriden Gap, a corridor of open country
which they are anxious to preserve. It thunders with main
roads and railways and has been bitten at by Birmingham
Airport and the National Exhibition Centre. The HoEW
and the tiny, polluted River Blythe run through it like
mute protests.

From Meriden the HoEW follows field paths with two ponds, then a rough track to Berkswell. You enter this delectable English village through a small wood and the churchyard. Opposite is an ancient well where monks from Lichfield baptised their first converts. Nearby are stocks and a cattle pound and in front of the Bear Inn is a cannon captured in the Crimean War. The present Church of St John the Baptist is mainly Norman and Early English but there are contributions from most other periods. The crypt and much of the nave and chancel are Norman, see the round arched windows. The tower is late 15th century and the half timbered vestry over the main door is from 1611. The squat tower has a peal of six 15th and 16th century bells, there is a superb 17th century candelabra and some rather fine stalls from 1909. Go and see, get the informative colour illustrated booklet, and make sure you leave lots of money.

The Way leaves Berkswell through the church garden and the park of the Berkswell Hall with its lake, the end of which you cross on a wooden causeway.

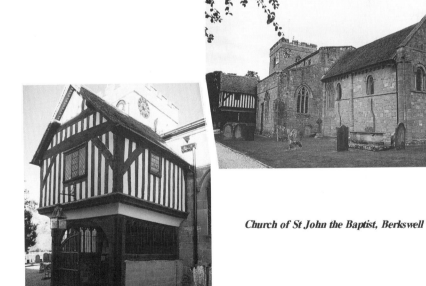

Church of St John the Baptist, Berkswell

(S117) Take 1st lane L 400yds to sharp L bend. Take drive ahead & round R bend to gates. Go L past pond & via gate to field.

(S118) Head for bottom R field corner to cross plank & stile. Follow R hedge to crest & cross stile. Go ahead parallel with L hedge to cross bottom stile.

(S119) Bear L & cross midhedge stile. Follow R hedge to stile & road. Cross & go L to pub.

Balsall Common

Balsall Common

(N166) Stand at end of lane with pub on your R. Go L 200yds to double power pole with gizmo & cross stile beneath.

(N167) Follow L hedge & cross stile. Keep same line over plank bridge to cross stile. Go up parallel with R hedge & cross field top stile.

(N168) Follow L hedge down to cross stile & plank. Head for R end of trees ahead & take gate.

(N169) Go ahead to drive & R to entrance. Go ahead 350yds to T junction. Go R to A452.

◄

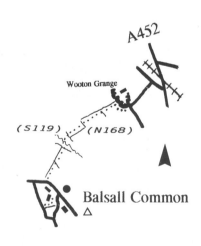

BERKSWELL

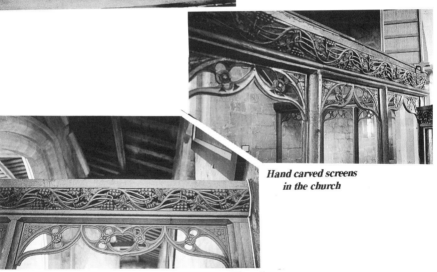

Hand carved screens
in the church

Berkswell Park

(68)

(S120) Take lane by pub 75 yds (past house) to power pole. Cross stile R, go to bottom L field corner & cross stile to lane

(S121) Go L past farm & cross stile R. Go ahead round field edge to projecting fence corner.

(S122) Go ahead, bearing R to L of midhedge, & cross BRIDGE. Go ahead to cross stile, keep same line (via midhedge stile) to top field corner, & cross stile.

(S123) Go L down hedge (via stiles) to field corner with building R. Go L into thicket & follow path to lane.

(S124) Go R 50yds & take track L. Follow .4 mile & pass farm R to field.

(S125) Go ahead midfield & up to meet hedge corner. Follow hedge to tree clump & go thro to field. Go up L & cross corner stile.

(S126) Go L & cross high stile. Go R by hedge 3 for fields & cross corner stile. Pass 2 oaks to stile & lane.

(N158) Go L by hedge (via stiles) to field corner & cross high stile L

(N159) Follow R hedge 100yds & cross stile R. Follow R hedge 100yds & take path thro thicket to field. Go L down hedge to its corner.

(N160) Keep ahead to join track, & follow .4 mile to lane

(N161) Go R 50yds to just past drive L. Take path L thro thicket to field.

(N162) Follow R hedge (via 2 stiles) & cross summit stile R.

(N163) Follow R hedge & cross stile. Go ahead (projecting hedge on your R) & cross stile.

(N164) Go ahead & cross bridge. **Sight black & white house** & aim 100 yds L, to projecting fence corner. Follow L field edge to lane.

(N165) Go L 80yds & cross stile R. Follow R hedge to end. Bear L to midhedge stile & lane. Go L to

Balsall Common

Balsall Common

Oldwich Lane

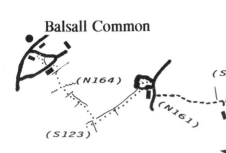

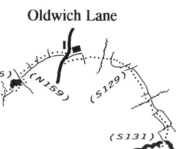

(N164)

(S126)

(N159)

(S129)

(N161)

(S123)

(S131)

Chadwick End

A4177

*Chapel of the Knights Templar,
Temple Balsall*

Pond and hedge at Wootton Grange

From Berkswell Park the HoEW crosses the A452 Warwick - Brownhills road and another railway. This one is the famous London & Birmingham Railway built by George and Robert Stephenson. The Way has been level since it entered Berkswell but now, after a lane, it starts to rise and fall gently and will do so all the way to Alcester.

At Balsall Common the HoEW passes the Saracens Head Inn. On the old painted sign the saracen was a truculent fellow wearing a coal scuttle and looking scornful. The new metal sign has a wizened old chap who might stand you an orange juice. The pub is 13th century and its connection with the crusades lies a mile south-west at the Hall, chapel and almshouses of the Knights Templars.

There is lots more I could tell you about Balsall Common but the village is a mile east so it would all be wasted. As the Way leaves the lane at the back of the pub it passes two handsome houses. Magpie Cottage on a bend is a gem of timber frame building, while Balsall Common Farm is graciously proportioned brick.

The long succession of pastures and stiles with a few arable fields continues, crossed by just two lanes. At Fen End you will meet a thorn thicket. The HOEW Wardens clip it regularly but expect a few prickles. I mention this because there is nothing much else at Fen End, the HoEW could be miles from anywhere. From a minor road the Way follows a long farm track down to cross a valley, then up a field edge and through a thicket. In past editions have I mentioned a ruined cottage here, though walkers tell me it can't be seen. Anyway, I liked it because it made me think of Mr Fox in *Jemima Puddle Duck* who lived in a *"dismal retired house amongst the fox gloves"*, and I have always wanted to see one.

The paths level off again now as the HoEW crosses grazing land to Oldwich Lane. After another field the route falls sharply to a footbridge to cross a small bog. This is caused by the simple fact that the stream has very little fall. For years walkers splashed across, and in winter this could be a memorable experience. However in 1994 Warwickshire County Council built the bridge because, as part of the HoEW, the path is heavily used.

Over a crest, then a stream, a couple of fields and a wood, and the Way enters Chadwick End, rather furtively, round the back of the some garages.

A few fields later you pass through a stable yard to meet a lane and pass on your left the Poor Clares Convent. This Franciscan house established in 1793 was rebuilt around 1870 in French Gothic style.

Baddesley Clinton Manor

Pool in the grounds

Stratford Canal

(72)

(S127) Go R a few paces & take stile L. Go L heading 60yds R of houses, to cross stile.

(S128) Bear R down to cross bridge. Cross next stile. Go half R past power pole & cross stile in R hedge.

(S129) Go ahead & cross stile. Follow L hedge over crest & cross stile, then down & cross bridge.

(S130) Go parallel to L hedge & take gateway. Follow narrow field & take gate. Bear R to where R hedge meets wood.

(S131) Take steel tube stile & follow wood path (ignore L fork) to field. Follow L hedge & cross stile.

(S132) Go L & pass garage doors to road. Bend L & pass next garage doors on your R. Go thro posts to A4141.

Chadwick End

Chadwick End

(N150) HoEW crosses road 100yds UPHILL from Orange Tree pub Take track by house No 1.

(N151) Follow to yard & go L thro steel posts. Pass garages L, then bear R to pass more. Take path L by fence & cross stile.

(N152) Go ahead with hedge on your R into wood. Exit via stile to field corner.

(N153) Cross diagonally & take gateway L. Follow L hedge & take gate. Go parallel with R hedge to cross bridge.

(N154) Go up & cross stile. Follow R hedge over crest & down to cross stile.

(N155) Go ahead (hedge on your R) & cross stile. Bear L past power pole & cross stile. Cross bridge.

(N156) Go up to 60yds L of first house & cross stile. Go ahead bearing R past houses & stile. Cross next stile R to lane.

(N157) Go R a few paces & take recessed stile in L hedge. Go ahead past oaks to projecting hedge corner & take stile. ◀

Chadwick End

(S133) HoEW crosses road 100yds UPHILL of Orange Tree pub. From house No 3 (antique shop) take stile opposite.

(S134) Follow hedge & cross stile. Follow L hedge (via stiles & gates) thro stables to lane.

(S135) Go R, pass lane R & on 400yds to ornate gate post. Cross stile R & follow fenced path to drive.

Baddesley Clinton

ALTERNATIVES

Route (B) is the original line of the Way. It is quite green and pretty with a fine church at Rowington. However it has been badly marred by the M40 and involves some 1.25 miles of road walking. Route (A) is an off road alternative via a very attractive canal junction and the Stratford Canal.

SOUTHBOUND (A) pg 75

SOUTHBOUND (B) pg 79

NORTHBOUND (A) pg 76

NORTHBOUND (B) pg 80

Routes (A) & (B) meet

(N147) From where Manor drive splits in two, walk away from house & take kissing gate R.

(N148) Follow fenced path 600yds to lane. Go L, pass lane L & enter farm gate L.

(N149) Follow thro stables to field. Follow R hedge (via gates & stiles), then L hedge to A4141.

◄ Chadwick End

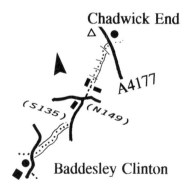

Baddesley Clinton

Route (A)

(SA136) From where drive to Manor splits in two, cross stile on field side.

(SA137) Look at house, then wood on its R & aim for wood's R end. Go with fence/hedge on your L .3 mile (via stiles) to field with pylon & red shed.

(SA138) Cross diagonally to L end of red shed & cross stile to yard. Go ahead, exit via stile, & follow track to B4439.

TRAFFIC - GREAT CARE

(SA139) CROSS ROAD HERE & go R on verge 200yds to opposite pub. Go L onto towpath.

(SA140) Go ahead to canal junction & turn R. Pass under railway, pass path L & cross footbridge to reach fingerpost.

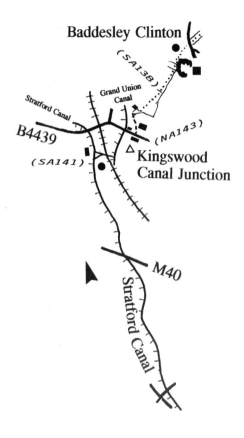

Baddesley Clinton

(SA138)

Grand Union Canal

Stratford Canal

B4439

(SA141)

(NA143)

Kingswood
Canal Junction

M40

Stratford Canal

Kingswood Junction

(SA141) From fingerpost pass Waterways Office & skirt basin to 1st lock, then cross bridge.

(SA142) Follow canal 1.8 miles to Lock 30 & Bridge 40. Exit L to lane & go R to T junction.

next para (S145)

Route (A)

(NA138) Take lane opposite to cross canal bridge & go down L to join towpath. DO NOT GO UNDER BRIDGE.

(NA139) Follow Stratford Canal 1.8 miles to & Lock 22. Cross bridge & skirt basin past Waterways Offices to fingerpost.

Kingswood Junction

(NA140) From fingerpost follow GU Canal past lock & cross footbridge. Pass under railway to canal junction.

(NA141) Go L to first bridge & up to road. GREAT CARE - DO NOT CROSS.

(NA142) Go R on verge 200 yds to Manor House gate R.

(NA143) GREAT CARE. Take track opposite to end & cross stile to yard. Take stile R of brick shed. Cross field diagonally & take corner stile.

(NA144) Follow R hedge .3 mile (via stiles) to its corner. Keep same line & cross stile to drive.

Baddesley Clinton

NEXT - para (N147) pg (74)

Lock cottage on the Stratford Canal

Kingswood Canal Junction

The HoEW continues on a lane, then a fenced path beside woodland. Look out for the wild plums. You arrive at the drive to Baddesley Clinton Manor from where you can see the house, one of the last perfect medieval manor houses. It has been National Trust property since 1940.

The first manor house was built in the 13th century but much of the present building dates from the 15th and 16th. For 500 years it belonged to the Roman Catholic Ferrers family and the greatest influence on the structure was Henry Ferrers (1549 - 1633). During his 70 years as squire he installed most of the panelling, chimney pieces and armorial glass, and built the Great Hall in the 1580's.

Uncommon features of the house include the obvious and beautiful moat, and some ingeniously concealed priest holes; very necessary for a pious Roman Catholic family in the late 16th century. In its early years the house was the scene of murder and tragedy. The founder of the Manor was John Broome, Under Treasurer of England, who was murdered in 1468. His son Nicholas waylaid the killer in 1471 and "slew him". Later he entered the parlour at Baddsley to find the parish priest "chocking" his wife under the chin, so he slew him as well. In those days they did not mind you slaying one or two people so long as you kept it within reason, so Nicholas got off with a couple of penances.

There is a tradition of ghosts at Baddesley, including that of the priest who was probably not too happy about the penanace business. He takes vestments out of one box and places them on another. There has been an unidentified lady who sat in the library, solemn and mournful footsteps that try door handles, an army officer, sounds of rapping and tearing cloth, a very pretty young lady in black and a sad lady. Excellent eyewitness accounts were written by the talented and entertaining Rebecca Dulcibella Dering, a 19th century descendant. Read about it in *Midland Ghosts & Hauntings* published by QuercuS which has an advert at the front of this book and turns out, ahem, to be me.

ROUTE A follows field paths to Kingswood Canal Junction where the Stratford and Grand Union Canals pass and are linked by a spur. The locks, cottage, basins and iron bridges make an attractive group.

The Stratford starts at Kings Norton, Birmingham where it leaves the Worcester & Birmingham Canal. It has 55 locks on its winding way to Stratford, unusual white drawbridges and unique barrel roofed cottages. The Stratford was built in the early days of modern civil engineering and follows river valleys and contour lines to avoid large earthworks. This is why it meanders through the meadows and skirts little hills.

The Grand Union links London with Leicester, Nottingham and Birmingham. This section leaves Birmingham via Solihull and after the junction heads down Hatton Locks to Warwick. The GU is a later canal with long tunnels, deep cuttings and huge embankments. It cut quite directly through the land-scape so boats could travel faster and cheaper. If the Stratford is a poet's canal, the GU is an accountant's.

ROUTE B follows a tree lined path to the isolated parish church of St Michael. In spring the churchyard is bright with daffodils and bluebells. The nave is 13th century with additions in the next two centuries by Nicholas Broome as part of his penances. The chancel was rebuilt and extended in the early 17th century and the whole place was restored in the 19th. Go and see the triple locked wooden chest in the nave which once held parish cash, the unique Sarah Green Chamber Organ of 1797 and the east window.

The Way to Rowington is very green and the hills get hillier. You approach St Lawrence's church uphill and for the second time the Way passes through a churchyard. The plan and some of the church's fabric is Norman, but the building is most impressive as you approach because of the strength of that squat tower. Inside the interesting feature is the glass. There is a fine west window, high quality Victorian glass by William Kempe and an east window with medieval glass.

Baddesley Clinton
Route (B)

(SB136) Find where drive to Manor splits in two & follow either fork. Pass car park & take path L. Pass church to gate & track.

(SB137) Take next gate & go sharp R onto path. Follow .75 mile on same line, via stile, gates, bridge & track. Where track bends R to farm, fork L to lane.

(SB138) Go L .3 mile & take gate R, opposite Green Farm.

(SB139) Cross midfield to gate & take stile on its R. Bear L to tree at L end of opposite hedge.

(SB140) Pass projecting hedge corner & go with hedge on your R to take gate. **SIGHT on skyline ahead flat hedge from R then trees begin.** Go ahead to 1st tree & cross stile. ◀

(SB141) Follow L hedge (then line of trees, then hedge) to cross stile. Go ahead & cross top L corner stile.

(SB142) Cross field top & take stile to church. Go R to gate & B4439.

(SB143) Go L a few paces & take lane R. Cross canal & join track R.

(SB144) Follow R field edges to radio mast. Take track R to lane. Cross M40 & go .6 mile (past junction R) to T junction.

next para (S145) ▶

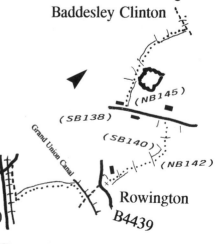

(79)

Route (B)

(NB138) Take lane opposite .6 mile (past lane L) & cross M40.

(NB139) Just after, go R up track to crest. Go L on field edges .3 mile & round R corner to lane.

(NB140) Go L to B4439. Go ahead & cross to churchyard. Pass church on your R & cross stile in L hedge.

(NB141) Cross field top & take stile. Go R down hedge, cross stile, & keep same line to cross corner stile. ◄

(NB142) Go ahead to where 3 hedges meet & take gateway. Go with hedge on your L to its corner.

(NB143) Bear L to cross stile L of gateway. Cross midfield to gate & lane.

(NB144) Go L .3 mile & take gate R by double power pole with gizmo.

(NB145) Follow path (becomes track) past wood. Take small gate & keep same line .5 mile (via gate, bridge & stiles) to track.

(NB146) Go L (via gates) to pass church & go R to drive.

Baddesley Clinton

◄NEXT - para (N147) pg (74)

Rowington church with tombs

Routes (A) & (B) meet

(S145) Take lane opposite 200yds & cross stile R. Go upfield with power lines (via stiles) to brick wall & track.

(S146) Go R to gates/stiles. Go L up wood edge. Cross stile & pass thro wood to field.

(S147) Go R to track. Go L via gate, round R bend & take gate.

(S148) Go L .3 mile to lane. Go R, round bend, & enter farm drive R.

(S149) Go ahead & take gateway. Bear L to follow hedge & cross 2 stiles into field.

(S150) Go half L to 1st oak in L hedge. Follow hedge & cross corner stile

(S151) Go L round field corner, pass thro copse & cross stile. Bear L to projecting hedge corner, then up R field edge to track.

(S152) Cross field bearing L & enter hedge gap. Go ahead thro thicket, take L fork & exit R via stile.

(S153) Cross to far L corner & take stile. Go L 450yds, cross stile & go half R to bottom of dip.

(S154) ROW circles R round breast of hill. We advise permissive route over crests, then down to iron gate onto road. Go ahead to main street.

Henley in Arden

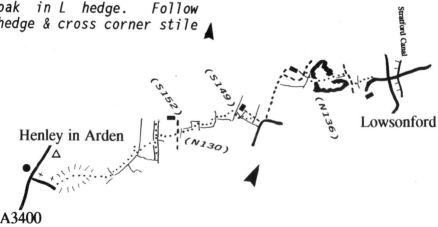

Henley in Arden

(N127) Put your back to White Swan & go R to corner church. Take lane L to its end & take iron gate.

(N128) ROW cirles L round breast of hill. We advise permissive path over crests & up bank to stiles. Cross stile L & follow ridge 400yds, to cross stile R.

(N129) Bear L & cross midhedge stile. Go L then 1st R to field. **Sight power poles ahead** *& aim between pole with gizmo & next L, to meet track.*

(N130) Cross into field & go down with L hedge to its corner. Bear L & cross stile to copse.

(N131) Go thro, then follow R hedge round field corner, & cross stile under tree.

(N132) Follow R hedge to last oak. Bear L to R end of cyprus trees & cross stile. ◀

(N133) Cross next stile & ◀*follow R hedge, bearing L to join track to lane.*

(N134) Go L, round R bend & take track L. Cross bridge & take next gate R.

(N135) Follow track round L bend & take gate. Go R, follow wood 25 yds & enter gap L.

(N136) Go thro & cross stile. Go ahead to take gates etc. Go R to end of brick wall.

(N137) Cross stile L, pass power pole & cross bottom stile. Aim L of house & cross stile. Take lane L to road.

ALTERNATIVES

see note on page *(74)*

◀

(82)

ROUTE A follows the Stratford Canal to a lane at Lowson-ford. ROUTE B leaves Rowington to enter our transport museum section. In turn it crosses the Grand Union Canal (1800-1820), the North Warwickshire railway line (1850), the M40 (1990) and Stratford Canal (1793-1815).

The routes meet and follow a lane, then a field path up to an oddly functionless brick wall. Look at the base and you will see that it was a railway bridge over a link to the North Warwicks line. You meet another bridge and cutting later.

The land rises a little as the Way plunges into a conifer wood to emerge on a track at Coppice Corner Farm. The rest of the route to Henley in Arden is through small hills, very green and attractive, with views of distant woods.

You enter and cross a thicket with paths. This is Edge Lane which should be a path or track lightly garnished with trees. It is an old road about two miles long which follows the edge of an escarpment, one of the most interesting and attractive landscape features in mid Warwickshire. There are long views over Henley in Arden to the Alne Hills.

The valley before you is that of the River Alne, a tiny tributary of the Arrow and the Avon. It rises north-east of Redditch, and though not a big river it has flooded Henley. Commissioners reported in 1548 to Edward VI; "... *a brook which in winter so riseth that none may pass over it without danger of perishing,...* ". Downstream it is captured to form an ornamental lake at Wootton Hall.

You enter Henley across "The Mount", obviously a fort-ification. The earthworks are attributed to Thurstan de Montfort in the 11th century but like many similar prominent hills, one can imagine very much earlier occupation. Sensible military men naturally build on the experience and structures of their predecessors, and though Iron Age generals may not have commanded sophisticated weaponry, their defensive structures seem impeccably logical.

From The Mount you pass the church of St Nicholas before following the lane to the town centre and the church of St John the Baptist. On the way you cross the insignificant River Alne which separates the two parishes of Henley and Beaudesert and explains the need for two churches. In fact they have been effectively the same town since a market charter of 1220. The stump of a 15th century market cross stands in the centre, one of very few left in the county. There will be one fewer if it shrinks any more.

Henley in Arden can claim to be the heart of the Heart of England Way and capital of Arden. The character of this little market town appears in its wide main street, a quaint, comfortable, harmonious mixture. Timber framed buildings sit beside red brick and tile, grand stone 18th century ones beside early and mid Victorian. The roofs are very rewarding, castellated, gabled, with classical parapets or plain eaves. The Guildhall is 15th century and since 1915 has housed the revived sittings of the manorial Court Leet and Court Baron which appoint various officers for the manor. This court is exempt from a 1976 Act of Parliament abolishing extinct courts.

The Guildhall

HENLEY IN ARDEN

(84)

(S155) Face White Swan & take lane on its R. Pass car park & follow path past end of street to road

(S156) Take path opposite, cross railway & follow fenced path to cross stile. Bear L down field to cross MIDHEDGE bridge.

(S157) Go with hedge on your L & cross stile. Keep same line towards house ahead, & cross stile to A4189.

(S158) Enter drive of house opposite, take brick stile & go ahead to cross stile. Go length of narrow paddock & cross stile.

(S159) Go half L to field bottom & cross stile. Go through dingle & cross footbridge.

(S160) Go half R past post & cross stile. Keep same line (via 2 stiles) to crest by watertank.

(S161) Go ahead a few paces & (when in view) head for middle of bottom hedge & cross stile. Go ahead & cross stile, then bear R to join hedge.

►

(N121) Take small gateway opposite, follow L hedge 450yds & cross corner stile. Bear R to 150yds R of field corner & cross stile. Go ahead midfield to cross next stile.

(N122) Bear R to top field corner by water tank. Cross stile & go half R to cross stile. Go half L & cross stile. Go ahead to field corner & cross footbridge.

(N123) Go through dingle & cross stile to field. Go half L & cross stile. Go ahead & cross stile, then brick stile, to B4189.

(N124) Take stile opposite & cross crest midfield, to take stile recessed in far hedge.

(N125) Follow path & cross bridge. Follow L field edge to top L field corner, cross stile & follow path over railway to road.

(N126) Go L 25 paces & take steps opposite. Pass end of road & go through car park to

Henley in Arden

◄

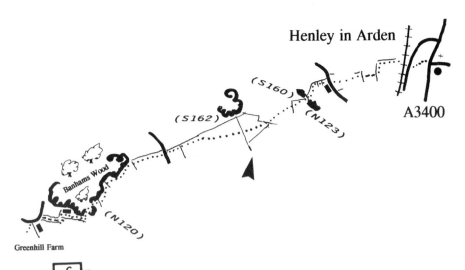

Henley in Arden

A3400

Banhams Wood

Greenhill Farm

(S162) Follow R hedge .5 mile to lane.

(S163) Cross stile opposite & follow R field edge up to cross stile. Go with wood on your R .5 mile (via 2 gate/stiles) into section with bushes L, & take small gate.

(S164) Follow clear path (bending L) & exit to field corner.

(S165) Take small gate R, follow L fence (past gate) & cross stile. Go on to corner & take small gate L to track.

(S166) Go R to gate & cross ladder stile to lane. Go L round bend & take double iron gate L. Go half R down field to cross stile & bridge.

(N118) Go R across gateway to gate, & cross ladder stile. Follow track 170yds & take small gate L.

(N119) Go R on field edge (via stile) & take small gate. Go L into wood by fence. Follow clear path (bends R) & take small gate.

(N120) Go with wood on your L .5 mile (via 2 gate/stiles) & cross stile. Follow L fence down to lane.

(86)

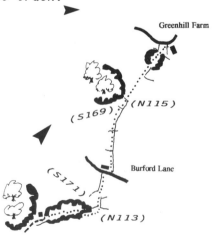

(S167) Follow path thro thicket (follows line of L fence) to stile & field.

(S168) Follow L hedge via 2 stiles & on 80 yds to hedge corner. Keep same line over long field to take wood corner gate.

(S169) Bear L & take small gate/stile by oak. Follow L hedge .5 mile to lane.

(S170) Go R 100yds & take 1st gate L. Follow R hedge till it bends R, then keep same line & cross corner stile.

(S171) Bear R PAST projecting wood corner, then with trees on your R take gate. Pass thro wood & exit on track, curving R past brick shed to track.

(N111) Ignore gateway/gap ahead & curve L on sunken track. Take gate & go thro wood to gate.

(N112) Go with wood edge on your L to its end, then ahead to field corner.

(N113) Take L stile & follow R hedge to its corner. Keep same line, bearing L to join L hedge & follow to gate & lane.

(N114) Go R 100yds to lane junction. Take path L & stile into field. Go with hedge on your R 3 fields, then to wood CORNER gate (not gate into wood).

(N115) **Put your back to gateway & sight far hedge. Look just L to big hedge gap with pylon just above R,** & head for it.

(N116) Meet projecting hedge corner R & keep same line (via stiles) to thicket.

(N117) Go thro, cross bridge & stile. Go up to top L corner gate & lane.

Greenhill Farm

(N115)

(S169)

Burford Lane

(S171)

(N113)

The walk between Henley and Alcester is one of the best parts of the Heart of England Way; hilly, wooded and pastoral. After crossing the railway (the Birmingham to Stratford line, once GWR), the route to Greenhill Farm is almost straight. A small kink south at Hunger Hill dives through a little dingle with a bridge and a nice pond. Next comes a viewpoint on a hill with a mysterious set of water tanks, followed by a long field leading to Banhams Wood.

This hillside SSSI is only about 450 feet high but dominates the surrounding landscape. The permissive path round the southern edge of the wood was agreed specially to avoid having a Long Distance path through the flora and fauna. These are some of the best views on the HoEW and we are most grateful to the farmer who made it all possible.

At Greenhill Farm you turn south, tumbling down a little valley then up through a mighty thicket. The map calls it "pit (dis)", and it was one of the quarries which supplied stone for Alcester Town Hall. The Way follows a broad ridge past a wood and the seductively contoured Round Hill to the Alne Woods. They mark the end of the Alne Hills, and you start to descend with fine views south. An open, field edge section leads to a green lane running to the pleasing village of Great Alne. The Way crosses a big dome of land, passes a trig point and follows a leafy path into Alcester.

This compact little town is enthusiastically cared for by its citizens. Once a Roman staging post (Aluana), there are fine 15th and 18th century buildings. Most are in red brick but Malt Mill Lane shows timber undisguised and at its best. The mellow little "War Memorial" Town Hall was built in 1641 and bought by the townspeople to commemorate the 1914/18 War. St Nicholas's Church has a 14th century tower and you expect a medieval interior, but it is classically cool, light and sane with Tuscan columns. It holds the tomb of the dreadful Fulke Greville who amongst other foul deeds felled the oaks on Cannock Chase. Now he and his wife lie stiff and pious, hoping that no one from Rugeley or Cannock comes by.

(S172) Go L 400yds to lane. Go L 400yds (past white house) to L bend, & take stile R before cottage.

(S173) Follow L field edge past cottage & cross stile. Go ahead down to stile & track. Go R to lane.

(S174) Cross & go L a few paces. Take stile R, cross end of small field & take stile L.

(S175) Go R & round field corner, then with hedge on your R 350yds to mark post. Take hedge gap. Go with hedge on your L (then trees) & enter gap in trees to reach track.◄

(S176) Cross & take stile ◄ahead to field. Go R to bottom midhedge stile & road.

(S177) Cross & go L a few paces to take double gates. Follow hedge .6 mile (1st on your L then after stiles, on R) to stile & old railway.

(S178) Cross bridge & take stile. Cross next stile R. Go L of hollow to trig point, then on same line down to projecting trees. Take stile & path to B4089.

(S179) Go R .5 mile, cross river (Arrow) & bear L to town centre.

Alcester

Malt Mill Lane, Alcester

Alcester

(N103) From HoEW seat, pass Town Hall & leave on B4089 (Great Alne road). Cross River Arrow & go .5 mile to take path L opposite number 32.

(N104) Cross stile & head for crest & trig point. Pass hollow on your L to take stile. Go L via stile, bridge & stile, to field.

(N105) Follow hedge .6 mile (first on your L, then after stile, on your R) & (via stiles) to lane.

(N106) Go L a few paces & take stile R. Go to top L field corner & cross stile L to track.

(N107) Cross & exit to field. Bear R by trees (then hedge) 300yds to mark post. Take gap & go with hedge on your L. Round field corner & cross stile L. Go R to lane.

(N108) Go L a few paces & take track R. Cross cattle grid & take 2nd gate L.

(N109) Go up on green track & take gate/stile. Go with hedge on your R to lane.

(N110) Go L 400yds (pass white house) to take track R. Follow 400yds to pass sheds on your L.

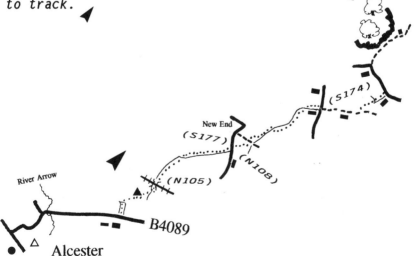

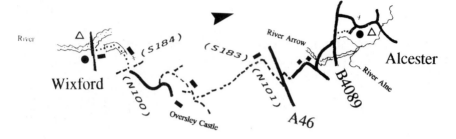

Alcester

(S180) From HoEW seat take Malt Mill Lane to end. Go R a few paces then L thro park to road.

(S181) Take lane opposite, cross bridge & take lane R to Primrose Lane L.

(S182) Go L 300yds. Cross A46 bridge & take STILE AHEAD to concrete track. Go up R, then L past silos

(S183) Follow track .5 mile to junction. Go R .3 mile to junction. Go L to pass gates L, & follow drive down to gates & junction.

(S184) Take track opposite, pass gates L & house R. Follow path past works & cross stile. Go with bank on your L & cross stile. Go thro caravans to pub & road.

Wixford

Wixford

(N99) Enter Fish Inn car park & take gate. Go ahead past caravans & cross 2 stiles. Follow path R & pass house L to lane.

(N100) Take drive opposite up to pass castle gates. Go L on track .3 mile (past track L & house L) to track junction. Go L .5 mile to farm.

(N101) Pass silos on your L & go R. Follow track to stile L & cross A422 bridge to lane. Follow to T junction.

(N102) Go R to road, then L over bridge to main road. Cross & follow path thro park to lane. Go R, round L bend, & up to square.

Alcester

River Arrow at Wixford

The HoEW leaves Alcester and crosses the River Arrow which has just absorbed the Alne. This marks the southern tip of the hilly triangle between Reddich and Henley, and of the Arden landscape. The Arrow flows south to join the Avon near Bidford, and the Way follows its valley as it flattens and opens into the Vale of Evesham.

From Primrose Hill there are fine views north towards the Lickey Hills and south to the Cotswolds. To the east is Oversley Wood, mainly conifers but Forest Enterprise are restoring native trees. It contains coppiced lime stools at least 1000 years old. To the west you can see the imposing classical front of Ragley Hall in its 400 acre park.

The Way follows long stony tracks across the plateau past Oversley Castle (genuine Victorian) and follows a drive lined with laburnums to a lane. This was the Roman Ryknild Street which ran north to Watling Street (A5) and south to Bourton on the Water and the Fosse Way. St Milburgha's pocket sized Church holds a brass of Thomas de Cruwe and his wife, one of the finest in the country.

⟨S⟩ Wixford

(S185) Take track opposite Fish Inn 100yds, cross bridge & stile. Go ahead on bank top (via bridge) to its end.

(S186) Go with hedge on your R (via stiles & gates) .3 mile to track. Cross stile opposite, then with hedge on your L (via stiles etc) to end.

(S187) Bear a little R, cross stile & go on to lane. Take lane opposite to main street. (Broom)

(S188) Take path opposite to sports field. Follow R hedge to lane.

(S189) Bear L & cross to follow fenced path past stile R, up to road.

(S190) Go R 250yds & cross road to opposite Broom Court Farm. Bear L & take fenced tarmac path.

(S191) Follow .5 mile (becomes lane) to L bend.

(S192) Go L 100 yds to post box. Take path opposite to B439. Take path opposite to street, go L to bridge.

Bidford on Avon

Bidford on Avon ⟨N⟩

(N90) From town side of bridge face town & go L 100 yds. Take track opposite to B439.

(N91) Take path opposite to road. Go L, round R bend & follow lane (then path) .5 mile to road.

(N92) Follow main road. Just before bridge, cross & go up to take path L.

(N93) Follow fenced path to lane. Take track opposite bearing R of hedge ahead.

(N94) Follow L hedge & then path to road.(Broom)

(N95) Take lane ahead to lane. Take track opposite (via stiles) to field.

(N96) Go ahead to L side of hedge & follow (via gates etc) to track.

(N97) Take gate opposite & follow L hedge .3 mile (via stiles etc) until ABREAST OF distant red farm R.

(N98) BEAR L via stile/ gate to join green bank. Follow via bridge, cross stile & take path to road.

◀ Wixford

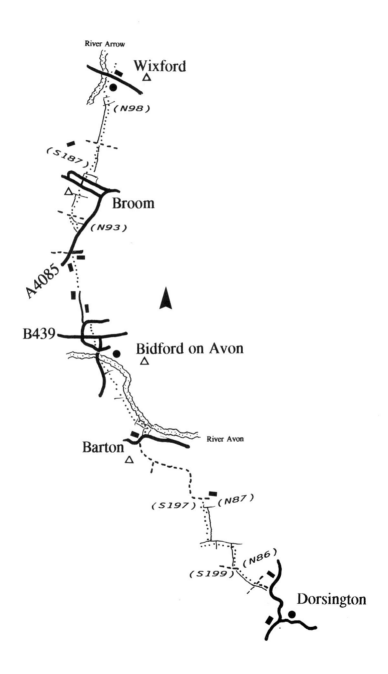

River Arrow

Wixford

(N98)

(S187)

Broom

(N93)

A4085

B439

Bidford on Avon

River Avon

Barton

(S197) (N87)

(N86)

(S199)

Dorsington

At Wixford you come to river level, the pub is The Fish, and for the next few miles the Way is willows and water meadows. The next village was called "Beggarly" Broom, because the people went in for basket making and knife grinding and traded as pedlars. It is a happy jumble of old and new houses including the 16th century timber framed and brick Broom Tavern.

Bidford on Avon's chief adornment and reason for existence is its many arched 15th century stone bridge which replaced earlier bridges and a ford once used by the Romans. The only historic building is the 13th century Falcon Inn at which Shakespeare once got very drunk. River traffic has increased since the Avon was made navigable to Stratford, and Bidford is now a small resort with tea shops, pubs and antique shops. However is has had baleful effects on water quality, wildlife and waterside plants.

Broom

Bidford on Avon's bridge

The weir at Barton

From Bidford the HoEW crosses wide green meadows beside the Avon to the lock and weir at Barton. Upstream, boats can join the Stratford Canal, and downstream at Tewskesbury they can sail north up the Severn or south on the Gloucester & Sharpness Canal to the Severn estuary. Barton has fine old buildings; most people notice the "Cottage of Content" pub but do look at the others in the local red brick and timber.

A long stony track leads up from the Avon through acres of fruit and veg to Barton Farm. This is fine, friable, fertile soil. However, in the wet it has the property of clinging to boots and not coming off again, causing rapid gains in height and weight and eventual immobility.

Dorsington is old and calm and sleepy. A grand oak girdled by a seat shelters a small green and behind is the 18th century red brick church of St Peter. But the nearby farm has a moat - rural England was not always peaceful.

Bidford on Avon

(S193) Cross Avon to south side & cross stile L.

(S194) Bear R to pass midfield power pole on your L & cross stile. Keep same line & cross hedge corner stile.

(S195) Go ahead to double power pole with gizmo. Cross stile & follow path to road. (Barton)

(S196) Go ahead up to R bend. Take track ahead .6 mile (past track R & sheds R) to farm.

(S197) Pass 1st shed R & go R to water tank. Go L, round field corner, & down with hedge on your L thro gap.

(S198) Go L (hedge on your L) thro 2 hedges to 3rd. Go R with hedge on your R to field corner. Go ahead to green track.

(S199) Go L & cross stile, then R up hedge to gate & track. Go L & round R bend to road.

(S200) Go R 500yds to village.

Dorsington

Dorsington

(N83) At village green face church & go R to T junction.

(N84) Go R 500yds via R bend & L bend. Go to next (R) bend (red roofed house ahead) & take gate L to track.

(N85) Follow fenced track & bend L to 3 gates. Take R gate & go with hedge on your L to bottom corner.

(N86) Cross stile L & go 8 PACES. Go R to field & with hedge on your L to corner. Go L (via 2 hedges) & take 2nd wide gap R. Go with hedge on your R to farm.

(N87) Go L & thro buildings to track. Go L .6 mile to road. (Barton)

(N88) Go ahead to R bend. Take lane ahead to stile & river. Go L & cross stile.

(N89) Go with hedge on your R to its end, then keep same line & cross stile. Bear R & head for bridge.

◄ Bidford on Avon

⟨S⟩ Dorsington

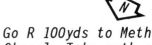

(S201) From seat · on village green face church & go L. Follow lane 250 yds, cross small bridge & take stile R.

(S202) Follow R field edge/stream .5 mile to end of fenced track. Go on by stream to field corner & cross stile & bridge.

(S203) Bear L to middle of gappy hedge & cross stile. KEEP SAME LINE past 1st power pole then 2nd to field corner, & cross bridge.

(S204) Follow L hedge (via 2 gateways) to field corner. Bear L down narrow strip & take gate/stile.

(S205) Go L hedge by hedge & cross 2 stiles. Follow R hedge to field corner by house, cross stile R & take path to road.

(N77) Go R 100yds to Methodist Chapel. Take path on its R & cross stile to field.

(N78) Go L & cross 2 stiles. Follow R hedge to field corner.

(N79) Go R into green track & take gate/stile. Follow R hedge (via 2 gateways) & cross bridge.

(N80) Go half L & pass power pole on your L to hedge corner. Keep same line past next pole & cross midhedge stile.

(N81) Keep same line, pass power pole on your R to field corner & cross stile & bridge.

(N82) Follow L hedge/stream .5 mile (via fenced track) to lane. Go L to green at

Dorsington

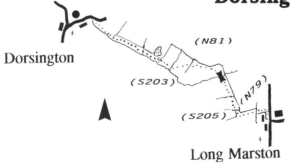

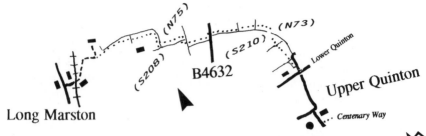

Long Marston   B4632   Lower Quinton   Upper Quinton   Centenary Way

Upper Quinton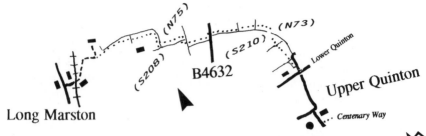

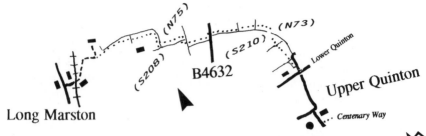

(S206) Go R & take 1st lane L. Follow 400yds (past L fork) & cross old railway.

(S207) Follow track, pass pond L & take gate. Go ahead to L bend. Keep same line .6 mile (via 2 stiles) to field corner. Go R & take corner gate.

(S208) Go with hedge on your R & cross corner stile R. Go L & thro 2 gates to gate & B4632.

(S209) Cross stile opposite. Go with hedge on your R (via 2 hedges) & cross steel bridge R.

(S210) Go ahead parallel with L hedge via 2 fields, & cross footbridge. Follow fenced path & cross bridge to road. Go R to junction.

(S211) Bear L & take lane opposite .4 mile to green at

Upper Quinton

Upper Quinton

(N70) Take lane across green AWAY from Meon Hill to T junction. Follow lane R & round L bend to cross roads.

(N71) Take Aylstone Close to its end & cross foot-bridge L. Follow fenced path & cross bridge.

(N72) Go ahead midfield to cross stile, & on to cross bridge.

(N73) Go L (hedge on your L) .4 mile (via gates) to B4632.

(N74) Take gate opposite. Go ahead via 2 gates & cross stile R. Go L with hedge & take gate.

(N75) Go R with hedge & round field corner. Go with hedge on your R .6 mile (via 2 stiles), then keep same line to track.

(N76) Go ahead .5 mile (via gates & old railway) to road.

(99)

From Dorsington the HoEW follows the line of the Noleham Brook to Long Marston. The landscape has this same level character for the next five miles to Upper Quinton and Meon Hill, the ground hardly rising above 130 feet. Many fields show traces of medieval ridge and furrow cultivation and there are hedges and ponds and willows. Depending on the light and time of day, these atmospheric trees can call to mind anything; jolly anglers, Mr Toad or witchcraft.

Charles II stayed at Kings Lodge in Long Marston on his journey south from Boscobel; he seems to have stayed almost everywhere in the Midlands. Near where the Way crosses the main road are the Masons Arms and St James's Church, which has a strange tower sitting on timber joists.

The HoEW crosses an old railway, once the GWR line which carried the Cornishman express from Birmingham via Stratford to Cheltenham. It was abandoned in 1976 and the District Council converted it to a cycling and walking route. It was here that I seemed to hear the whistle and thud of a steam engine, and knew I must be really ill when it went on. Eventually I found the cause on the nearby military base. An old but smartly restored little 060 pannier tank engine in LMS livery was puffing up and down an internal line hauling two quite incongruous Regional Railway coaches. I have no further explanation. Look out for the Sewage Fortress. Most Works look nautical but this one is distinctly military.

Soon you pass a disused airfield where they seem to have everything - car boot sales, powered model aircraft, go karts, and microlights. A succession of field paths brings you to Lower Quinton. There are two pubs, a pond and St Swithin's Church which is lofty and light, the first Cotswold stone church on the Way. There is a fine display of modern heraldic stained glass, some medieval fragments in a chapel and an incredibly complicated east window with lots of pink. The College Arms and Magdellen House beside it were named through an association with Magdellen College, Oxford. A lane leads from Lower to Upper Quinton with its spectacular green.

Upper Quinton

(S212) At green take lane towards hill. Pass lane L & go round R bend plus 50yds to L bend.

(S213) Take gate ahead & follow L hedge to cross stile. Keep same line to power pole & cross stile & bridge.

(S214) Bear L to join L hedge & follow it to cross stile L. Go R (hedge on your R) to cross stiles & track.

(S215) Go ahead past big trees, cross stile & plantation to field.

(S216) Go R & cross corner stile. Go L with hedge & take gate ahead. Bear R to hedge opposite (bottom of line of trees from L) & take gate.

(S217) Bear R, pass 50yds from projecting field corner & cross midhedge stile & bridge.

►

(N64) Go with fence on your L to cross bridge & stile. Bear L & pass 50 yds R of projecting field corner to take gate.

(N65) Bear L to hedge 80yds up from L field corner & take gate. Go with hedge on your R to cross corner stile.

(N66) Go up a few paces & take stile L. Go thro trees to field. Go ahead past two oaks to track.

(N67) Cross 2 stiles ahead & follow L hedge to cross stile L. Go R on field edge to near corner. Bear L to 80yds down hedge & cross bridge.

(N68) Go ahead midfield & cross field end stile. Go ahead to gate & lane.

(N69) Go ahead & round L bend to green at

◄ **Upper Quinton**

(S218) Go with fence on your R to join track & follow to B4632.

(S219) Cross stile opposite. Bear L & cross midhedge stile. Go L with hedge & take alley to B4632.

Mickleton

(N62) Take alley on R of butchers shop, follow R hedge & take corner stile R. Bear a little L to stile & B4632.

(N63) Take track opposite 400yds to L end of conifer row. Pass track L then pass sheds L. ▲

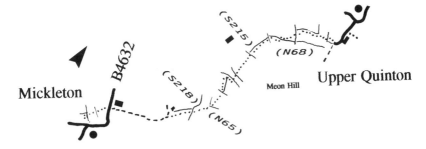

A coven of willows at Long Marston

(102)

⬠S Mickleton

(S220) At butchers shop face road & go L 30 paces to take lane opposite. Follow round R bend & take small gate.

(S221) Go with haha on your R & take small gate to churchyard. Exit via ramp to track.

(S222) Go L (via gate) to end of stone walls. Bear R to pass midfield oak on your R & take gate.

(S223) Go with hedge on your R & take gate. Go a few paces & cross stile R.

(S224) Enter field & bear L to pass projecting fence corner R. Go on to upper slope (with trees on your L) & take gate to lane.

(S225) Take path opposite to field. Go R by trees & take gate/gap into wood. Go thro to field. Go with hedge on your L to barn & lane. ▶

(N56) Enter gateway L & go R with hedge. Enter wood & follow path to field.

(N57) Go L, round field corner & take small gate or stile L to lane.

(N58) Take gate opposite & go down beside wood. Keep same line past projecting fence corner L, to far corner.

(N59) Cross stile, go L (via gate) & follow L hedge to take gate. Pass midfield oak on your R & go between stone walls to gate & track.

*(N60) Go ahead & take church ramp **R**. Pass church on your R & take gate. Go with haha on your L to take gate.*

(N61) Follow track to B4632. Go L to bend & butchers shop.

◀**Mickleton**

(103)

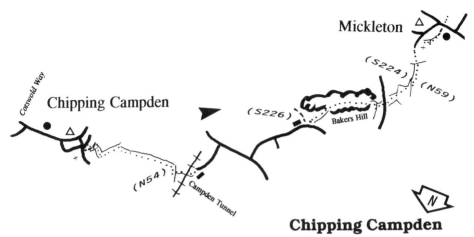

Mickleton

Chipping Campden

_(S226)_

Bakers Hill

_(S224)_

_(N59)_

_(N54)_

Campden Tunnel

Cotswold Way

N

Chipping Campden

(N51) From Town Hall pass arcaded Market Hall to road junction. Go R & pass church to bend & junction.

(N52) Take lane ahead 100 yds. Take path R to drive. Cross to L & take iron gate.

(N53) Follow fenced path to field. Go L on field edge to corner. Go R (hedge on your L) to bottom field corner.

(N54) Go R 25yds then L over 2 stiles. Follow R hedge, pass farm, & exit via gate.

(N55) Follow drive to lane. Go R & take next lane L. Follow .5 mile (past wood L) to black barn L.

S

(S226) Go R .5 mile to junction. Go R & take lane L.

(S227) Enter farm gate & pass front of house on your L, then with fence on your L (via 2 stiles) to field.

(S228) Go R, round field corner & with hedge on your R to corner. Go L with fence on your R to field corner.

(S229) Take path R to drive. Take path opposite to road. Go L & pass church on your L into

Chipping Campden

Are your eyes drawn mesmericly to the frowning bulk of Meon Hill? Does an unseen breeze strike a chill on warm days? I haven't noticed it either, but Meon Hill does have sinister associations with witchcraft. Anyway, at a height of nearly 600 feet it was an Iron Age fort and is the most northerly outpost of the Cotswolds.

The Way crosses the flank of Meon Hill then comes down into glasshouse country at Mickleton. From the main road this seems a flat, fertile, market garden sort of village, but as soon as you reach St Lawrence's Church and see the pastures and leafy hills beyond, you know that it is also in the Cotswolds.

The church of St Lawrence was started in the 12th century and enlarged in the 14th and 15th centuries. The 90 foot spire houses a ring of eight bells. The church was once left a charitable bequest (which failed) of £1,500 on condition that twelve boys, "none being short sighted or red headed", should sweep and garnish a tomb and pipe and fife around it.

The Way rises quickly to the beech clad ridge of Bakers Hill which it follows to Mickleton Hills Farm. Deep in a cutting near the house the Oxford - Worcester rail line shoots out of the Campden Tunnel. This was the scene of the Battle of Mickleton for three days in July 1851. The GWR was in dispute with the tunnel contractor and claimed possession of the works. The contractor stayed put so the engineer, Brunel, called up 2,000 navvies from other works and marched on the site. They were met by magistrates reading the Riot Act and police armed with cutlasses. General Brunel withdrew, marched up more men under cover of darkness and after the authorities had departed, took the tunnel. There was some fighting with fists and shovels and a few serious injuries. The contract dispute was referred to arbitration.

A rising field edge path brings the Way to Chipping Campden. A settlement has existed here since Saxon times, market town, wool town, crafts town and now visitors town. It was granted a charter in 1185 and later the right to hold several markets, which is the meaning of the name "Chipping". The wool trade brought staggering wealth to the Cotswolds. Most villages have magnificent churches and streets of fine stone buildings which are almost summed up in Chipping Campden's honey coloured High Street. The church buildings identify the years of prosperity because they were when the largest, most elaborate, additions were made. Most of them are in the richly elaborate architecture of the Decorated and Perpendicular periods from the late 12th century to the end of the 15th.

Chipping Campden declined to become an ordinary country town until the end of the 19th century, when a strange and unreal revival occurred. C R Ashbee, architect and designer, who had strong links with the Arts and Crafts movement brought his Guild of Handicrafts here, with 150 London craftsmen and their families. It was idealistic and based on high quality non essentials, so economically unlikely. The Guild failed in 1908 but the improvements it made to the town and the new railway links laid the foundation for its present role and prosperity.

St James's Church, Chipping Campden

From Baker's Hill

Chipping Campden

(S230) From Town Hall (not arcaded Market Hall) take arch under Noel Arms. Go thro car park & wall gap.

(S231) Go ahead up lane & pass sports field R to road.

(S232) Step ONTO track L & go immediately R. At end of hedge, keep same line to fork by low wall. Go R & take small gate.

(S233) Go R, cross drive & take small gate. Follow path to lane. Go R to church. ►

(N48) Pass church on your R, follow lane to end & take walled path L. Take small gate & cross drive. Follow L fence & take small gate.

(N49) Go ahead to end of low wall & fork L to end of hedge. Go with hedge on your L to track.

(N50) Step L onto path & go R. Pass sports field & on via lane, wall gap, pub car park & arch to

◄ **Chipping Campden**

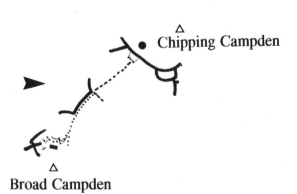

△
● Chipping Campden

►

△
Broad Campden

Broad Campden's church

Market Hall, Chipping Campden

*Heading for
Blockley*

(S234) Go ahead to ROAD BEND. Go R to end of wall L & take gate L.

(S235) Take next gate & follow wall L. Join line of trees to end.

(S236) Bear R to far top field corner & cross stile. Follow R hedge (count) 100 paces. Go R thro hedge.

(S237) Bear R to far top field corner BUT (when in view) head for top of railings.

(S238) Go with fence/wall on your R .4 mile (via stiles) to small gate R. DON'T TAKE IT.

(S239) Go down L & take small gate to track. Go L & round R bend to track junction.

(S240) Take 2nd track L .4 mile to L bend. Keep same line down hedge, go thro wood & take small gate. ▶

(N42) Take small gate L & follow path to field. Go up by L hedge, join track & go on .4 mile to track junction.

(N43) Take 2nd track R & round bend. Take small gate R before farm & follow path up to small gate. DON'T TAKE IT.

(N44) Go L by hedge/fence .4 mile (via 2 stiles) & along wall to end of railings.

(N45) Bear R to bottom corner where L fence meets gappy hedge. Cross gappy hedge & go with hedge on your L to cross stile.

(N46) SIGHT ahead/R narrow pointed turret & cross field (diagonally) towards it. When in view, head for projecting corner of trees

(N47) Go with trees on your R, then fence, then wall. Take gate to track & lane. Go R to junction & L to church. (Broad Campden) ◀

(S241) Go R into field, then L via 2 gates. Bear R & take field bottom gate

(S242) **SIGHT on crest ahead row of 5 trees.** Go to 2nd from L. Bear R to far R field corner & cross stile.

(S243) Go ahead via hedge gap to field. Go ahead midfield to L end of grey houses & cross stile. Go on to lane.

(S244) Go ahead 200yds to junction. Go L to village centre.

Blockley

Blockley

(N39) Take Bell Bank to top & go R to T junction. Take path ahead past house to stile & field.

(N40) Go ahead midfield to hedge gap by last tree. Go ahead & cross stile. **SIGHT row of trees** ahead & bear R to 2nd from R.

(N41) Go down & take bottom gate. Go up to top R corner & take 2 gates. Go ahead a few paces & enter gap R.

◄

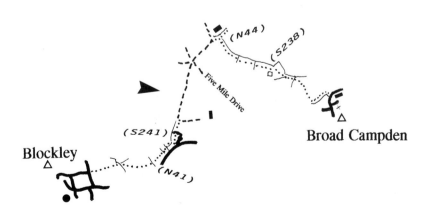

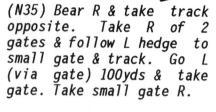

S Blockley

(S245) From foot of Bell Bank, go R 125yds & take lane L. Pass lane R & go up to road. Go L 75yds & take track R.

(S246) Follow to gate ahead & cross stile. Follow L hedge & cross stile.

(S247) Bear R past end of projecting garden & cross stile in projecting hedge corner.

(S248) Go up midfield between power poles, then head for top L field corner stile.

(S249) Go L on track 100yds & take gate. Go R by wall to gate & track. Go ahead to lane. ▶

(N35) Bear R & take track opposite. Take R of 2 gates & follow L hedge to small gate & track. Go L (via gate) 100yds & take gate. Take small gate R.

(N36) Take line between wall R & double power pole & (when in view) 50yds L of farm, to cross bottom corner stile.

(N37) Head past power poles to bottom field corner & cross stile. Follow R fence & cross stile. Take track to road.

(N38) Go up L to junction. Go R, round bend, pass lane L & up to street. Go R to cross roads.

◀ **Blockley**

BLOCKLEY

(S250) Bear R & take gate opposite. Go with wall on your L 500yds & go R to track.

(S251) Go L 400yds (CARE) to L bend when HOUSE comes in view 50yds ahead. Take SMALL PATH R & cross stile to field.

(S252) Go ahead to R side of lodge & take gate to drive. Bear R to end of hedge & small gate.

(S253) Path zigs ahead to far side of field, then zags back to drive 400yds on.

(S254) Follow drive to A44. Go R .4 mile to bus shelter at

Bourton on the Hill

Bourton on the Hill

(N32) From bus shelter go down A44 .4 mile to gates R & L. Go L on drive 400yds to stile R.

(N33) Path zigs diagonally to field corner, then zags back to lodge & drive. Take gate opposite lodge & go parallel with R fence. Cross stile & follow path to track.

(N34) Follow track L 400yds & take track R. Join wall & follow 500yds to lane.

◀

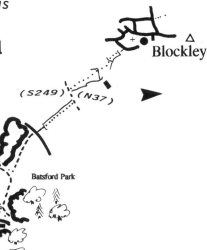

The HoEW leaves the town through a hotel yard and climbs gently over a big field to Broad Campden. If Chipping Campden is typical of the busy centres of the region, this little place pictures the sleepy domesticity of the tiny villages. Here is a Friends' Meeting House, a pub, a row of beautiful cottages and some larger houses. The pointy and narrow Victorian church is not really in keeping.

The next mile follows a path along the upper edge of a deep valley. As you move towards its head, the Cotswolds play their engaging trick of pretending they are in the northern uplands. The slopes are ragged with hawthorn and gorse and the only farming is rough grazing by brown and black cows. The plateau to the north though, is thoroughly farmed arable land like many higher areas in the Cotswolds. Turning south-east, the Way follows tracks past a quarry and down a huge hill. After a small thicket you emerge to the lip of an even steeper grass slope. This would give you boundless pleasure but for the fact the path leaps up the far side of this deep and beautiful valley to an even higher ridge.

After a couple of fields you are in Blockley, which lies on the edge of a hillside over the fast flowing Blockley Brook. The bowling green is the only level ground. The houses were built between the 16th and 19th centuries in a Cotswold stone that varies between strong ginger and pale cream. There were once twelve corn mills here in Blockley which in the 18th century were converted to silk throwing. A market had developed with the Coventry ribbon weavers and the water contained enough lime to give a fine sheen to the washed yarn. In the 1880s the millpond ran a dynamo to produce electricity and Blockley was one of the first villages in the country to have it.

The church of St Peter and St Paul has Saxon origins but the earliest surviving work is Norman. The are monuments, brasses, busts, effigies and marble tablets in memory of local families. Rock Cottage was the home between 1804 and 1814 of the prophetess Joanna Southcott, a Devon farmer's daughter and domestic servant who made mystical prophecies of vague catastrophe for the many and utopia for a chosen few. Her cult survived until the end of the 19th century.

The HoEW leaves Blockley on a path called the Duck Paddle and is soon climbing steeply through the hay to a green lane. If you are fit and do not need to pause because of the slope, turn and look at the view anyway. This hill is on a watershed, with streams on this side flowing to the Warwickshire Stour, the Avon, the Severn and the Bristol Channel. On the far side they join the River Evenlode and flow into the Thames.

Over the crest you continue beside the high wall of Batsford Park, part of which is an arboretum and garden centre. In the 1880s Lord Redesdale returned from a diplomatic posting in Tokyo with many Japanese plants and bronzes of Buddha, deer and a dragon, which now sits by a stream. He created a wild garden which was expanded to form the present arboretum in the 1920s by Lord Dulverton's family. There are huge and magnificent magnolias of over ninety species, Japanese conifers and spectacular maples, bamboo, cherry, tree of heaven and many others. You may not be able to carry plants from the garden centre in your rucksack, but you might cope with a cup of tea.

The Way takes an odd zig zag path from the arboretum but emerges on the A44. Next comes an uphill walk to Bourton on the Hill which seems much longer than it is. When you reach it there is not much of Bourton - a pub, a bus stop, a few houses, a phone box and the church of St Lawrence.

It was St Mary's until the 16th century and appears to have been rededicated by a clerical error. Anyway, there is an effigy of Larry and the waffle iron on which he was martyred over the north porch. Two Norman pillars are all that are left of the 11th century church; most of it is 12th century with a 14th century tower. The interior has been rather Victorianised but remains simple. There is a gorgeously ornate organ.

Bourton on the Hill

(S255) From bus shelter go UP & take lane L to phone box. Go R past timber sheds & take track L.

(S256) Take 2 gates to field. Go parallel with L fence & take gate. Follow L hedge, bearing R to cross stile under hedge tree.

(S257) Bear a little L & take midfence small gate. Take next gate. Go parallel with L fence heading for R end of CONIFERS ahead. Reach far field corner & take gate.

(S258) Take 2nd gate, go ahead & take next. Bear R, drawing closer to R fence to reach top field corner, & take gate.

(S259) Take 2nd gate & cross track. Follow R fence & take gate. Go with fence/hedge on your L .5 mile (via gates etc) to lane. Go L into

Longborough

Longborough

(N25) At War Memorial face church & go L 40yds to take gate R. Follow track then path thro allotments to small gate & field.

(N26) Go with hedge etc on your R .5 mile (via gates etc) to take gate by conifer wood.

(N27) Go thro & take gate. Follow L wall, cross track with cattle grid & take gate. Go ahead between walls to end.

(N28) SIGHT lake & head for L side. When in view, go to midfence gate. Go ahead via 2 gates (thro trees) to field.

(N29) Bear R to projecting wood corner. Bear L & go parallel with R fence 350yds, to take small gate

(N30) Take next gate. SIGHT L side of village & head for stile under hedge tree. Head for church tower (via gates) & join track to lane.

(N31) Go R to phone box, then up L to A44 & bus shelter R.

◄Bourton on the Hill

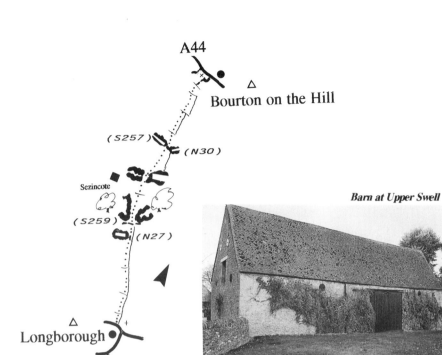

A44

Bourton on the Hill

(S257)

(N30)

Sezincote

(S259)

(N27)

Barn at Upper Swell

Longborough

Longborough

Donnington Brewery

(116)

⬡S⬡ Longborough

(S260) From War Memorial go DOWN & bend L to T junction. Go R 300yds & fork L past spring to junction.

(S261) Go L to sharp R bend & take track ahead. Follow to end & take gate/stile.

(S262) Bear R & follow R fence (via stile) to corner stile & field. Go ahead by trees to cross corner stile.

(S263) Follow path through trees up to field. Go on with trees on your L & cross bridge.

(S264) Go ahead parallel with R hedge & cross stile to track.

(S265) Go R 300yds to road. Take lane opposite. Pass lane R & turn next L. Follow .6 mile to B4077.

►

(N19) Go L (round R bend, pass lane L) to fork & take lane R. Follow .6 mile to T junction. Go R .4 mile (past lane L) to A424.

(N20) Take track opposite 300yds (past L fork) to end stile. DON'T CROSS IT - Cross stile L.

(N21) Go ahead (parallel with L hedge) & cross midhedge bridge.

(N22) Follow path ahead with trees on your R, then bearing R through trees & down, to cross plank bridge, then stile.

(N23) Go ahead past trees to fence corner & cross stile. Keep same line (via stile) to track & take gate. Follow to lane. Go ahead to junction.

(N24) Take lower lane past spring & follow road to T junction. Go L & round R bend to War Memorial.

◄ **Longborough**

(S266) Go ahead past lane L & round L bend. Go down 130yds & take small gate R

(S267) Take stile & cross field diagonally (via mid-fence stile) to top corner stile & path. Go R, take small gate & go ahead to small gate & field

(S268) Go ahead past midfield oaks to power pole. Bear R to far end of L fence, & take iron gate to drive.

(S269) Go R 500yds (past wood R) to 2nd L bend. Cross stile R

(S270) Head for L side of church & (when in view) double power pole with gizmo. Go L & cross stile.

(S271) Follow track round R bend to lane. Go L to War Memorial at

Lower Swell

Lower Swell

(N14) At bus shelter, face War Memorial & go L to road. Take lane opposite 100yds to No.4 & take track R.

(N15) Follow & cross end stile. Go ahead to end of wall & turn R. **SIGHT group of houses & lone one to L.** Head for L side of latter to stile & drive.

(N16) Go L 500yds (past last house L) & take iron gate L.

(N17) Go R to 2nd power pole from R. Go with fence on your L to field corner & take small gate.

(N18) Go ahead to corner & take gate. Go on a few paces & cross stile. Cross (via mid fence stile) to far bottom corner stile & path. Go L to B4077.

◄

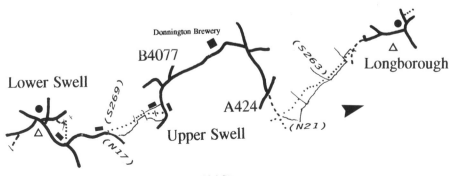

The HoEW leaves Bourton on the Hill across fields which were under strip cultivation until 1821. Passing through belts of woodland you enter the parkland of Sezincote and pass the front of this stately fantasy. The green Moorish onion dome and minerettes sit on a English classical house in warm golden stone, like a cheery old gent wearing a pantomime hat. It is all wonderfully mad and we need more of these.

The field edge route to Longborough is level and brings you out on a lane near the War Memorial. This is a typically attractive Cotswold village, though perhaps not in the first league of honey pots. Have a look at St James's church which has fifty of those rare survivors, medieval tiles, set around the base of a Victorian pulpit. These came from Hailes Abbey where English Heritage has managed to reconstruct several square yards of the old monastery floor. There are some jolly gargoyles, very large traceried windows to the nave and lots of other things, including a useful leaflet.

The HoEW follows Longborough's long main street, crosses more parkland and then climbs steeply to a green lane. Look back as you reach the crest. There are a couple more minor slopes, but the Way from here to Bourton on the Water has finished with hills and valleys and falls steadily.

There follows a good mile of lane, the second longest on the route. Happily, this is very quiet and pleasant with the attractive sight of the Donnington Brewery. They have no retail counter or bar, which seems a terrible shame.

Upper Swell is a tiny roadside settlement which you pass through quickly to cross a sloping field, pass a wood and join a driveway. The house, Abbotswood, is concealed in trees to the east. You walk past well manicured meadows trimmed with park railings and a lake. This is the lowest of three on the little River Dikler which flows south to join the Windrush. The first lake is at the brewery and the second above Upper Swell.

You enter Lower Swell up an attractive green slope heading for the church. Here is the last example of your faithful friend and guide, the *double power pole with gizmo*. Pay your respects and remember, some of us have to be useful rather than pretty. The village has a couple of pubs and restaurants, but the Way only passes through the end.

After a field track the route comes to a definitive drop past a wood to flat, green country which continues to the end. Passing Hyde Mill, you cross the River Dikler which looks clean and cressy and is rich with waterside flowers. The meadow beside it is managed for wild flowers and has a wonderful display of orchids. Please keep closely to the path, these places are rare and precious.

The HoEW reaches Lower Slaughter past the cricket pitch. The local team is also drawn from the village of Upper Slaughter and has the terrifying name of Slaughters United. Imagine their fast bowler thundering to the wicket to avenge a cheeky four. This village once featured in a Post Office advertisement, and certainly, the centre is quite beautiful with its tiny bridges over the River Eye. It is immaculate and personable but there is no shop and no pub and it feels like a hotelier presenting his professional face.

Bourton on the Water is one of the best known Cotswold villages and has a long history. The British (Celts) had a camp here, now cunningly camouflaged as a bed of nettles. The Romans had a religious shrine and a sort of transport cafe by their Fosse Way (A429 - ACCCCXXIX). For you there are all the pubs, tea shops and restaurants you could possibly desire at the end of the Heart of England Way. You could visit the motor museum, model village, model railway or birdland. The church of St Lawrence has many interesting features and a cupola like an early diving bell. But you might prefer just to wander down the main street between the golden houses and watch the River Windrush race under the 18th century stone bridges.

(S272) From War Memorial take main road UP past phone box & take lane L. Follow to last house & take track L.

(S273) Go ahead (fenced track) to L side of trees, then with trees on your R down to gate & bridge R.

(S274) Head for R side of farm ahead & via 2 gates to farm track. Go R & bend R to cross bridge.

(S275) Take small gate L. Go ahead to where trees meet hedge & cross stile. Keep same line via 2 gateways. Pass 25yds R of projecting fence corner, cross ditch & take gate in R hedge. ▶

(N10) Go L via gateway & pass 25yds L of projecting fence corner. Take 2 gateways & keep same line to kissing gate & bridge.

(N11) Go R on track past farmhouse to garages. Go L & take gate. Take next gate & keep same line to bridge & gate

(N12) Go with wood on your L to crest & take gate. Go ahead (fenced track) to farm. Take L of 2 gates & follow track to road.

(N13) Go ahead to T junction with B4068. Go R to junction & War Memorial

◀ **Lower Swell**

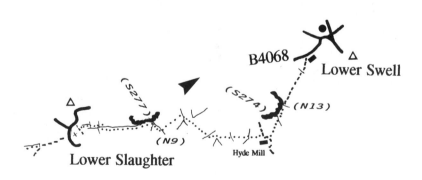

(121)

(S276) Bear L to pass 70 yds L of projecting fence corner & take gate in L fence. Go ahead to far field corner & take gateway.

(S277) Bear R over field corner to where hedge meets bushes & cross bridge. Go R & round corner, then on to near next corner & take gate R.

(S278) Go L by hedge, thro cricket ground & via paths to track. Go R to road.

(S279) Go L to junction (Lower Slaughter). Go L, cross road & take track R. Follow 300yds to its end & take gate.

Routes (A) & (B) join

(N6) Go L to junction. Go R (past church) to end of wall & take path R. Pass house L & take path L.

(N7) Go with hedge on your R thro cricket ground to field. Go on 200yds & take gate R.

(N8) Go with hedge on your L & round field corner to cross bridge. Bear L & take gateway.

(N9) Bear R, **SIGHT silo** & head R of it to take gate. Go R (70yds R of projecting fence corner) to field end. Take mid hedge gate.

Water, water at Lower Slaughter

(122)

Route (A)

(SA280) Follow tarmac path to A429. Cross, go R & take road L

(SA281) Follow 500yds to pass District Surveyors Office L & take path R.

(SA282) Follow to church & street. Go L to centre.

Route (B)

(SB280) Bear R with hedge on your R to small gate & lane. Go L 250yds & take stile L.

(SB281) Cross field diagonally down to far edge of wood. Cross stiles & go down to A429.

(SB282) Cross & take gate/ stile. Go ahead & cross old railway to path fork. Go L 400yds to church.

(SB283) Go R to street & L to centre.

Bourton on the Water

St James's Church

Bridges of Bourton

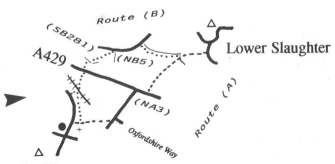

Bourton on the Water

(N1) From War Memorial follow main street to church. Enter churchyard & pass church to black & white posts.

ALTERNATIVES

Route (A) is the usual way to Lower Slaughter but there is rather a lot of road. I prefer quieter, more rustic Route (B).

Route (A)

(NA2) Go ahead on tarmac path 350yds to road. Go L .4 mile to A429.

(NA3) Go R 150yds & cross. Follow tarmac path .5 mile (via small gate) to street. (Lower Slaughter)

Route (B)

(NB2) Take path L (parallel to main street) 400yds to fork.

(NB3) Go R & cross old railway to field. Follow field edge to A429.

(NB4) Take stile opposite. Head for top R field corner & cross stiles. Cross field diagonally to top R corner stile & lane.

(NB5) Go R 250yds to 2nd tree clump R & take small gate R. Follow L hedge to tarmac path. Take gate & follow path to street. (Lower Slaughter)

◄ NEXT para (N6) pg (122)

Route (B)

(SB281)

A429

(NB5)

Lower Slaughter

(NA3)

Route (A)

Oxfordshire Way

Bourton on the Water